SETTING THE
CHRISTMAS STAGE

SETTING THE
CHRISTMAS STAGE

Readings for the Advent Season

JOHN INDERMARK

UPPER
ROOM BOOKS®
NASHVILLE

SETTING THE CHRISTMAS STAGE
Readings for the Advent Season

© 2001 by John Indermark
All rights reserved.

The Upper Room Web Site: http://www.upperroom.org

Scripture quotations not otherwise identified are from the New Revised
Standard Version of the Bible, © 1989 by the Division of Christian Education
of the National Council of the Churches of Christ in the U.S.A.
Used by permission. All rights reserved.

Scripture quotations designated KJV are from the
King James Version of the Bible.

Scripture quotations designated AP are the author's paraphrase.

Cover and interior design by Troy Ylitalo
Cover art by Justin Collett
First Printing: 2001

Library of Congress Cataloging-in-Publication
Indermark, John, 1950–
    Setting the Christmas stage: readings for the advent season / by John Indermark.
        p. cm.
    ISBN 0-8358-0947-1
    1. Advent—Prayer-books and devotions—English. I. Title
BV40 .I48 2001
242'.332—dc21   2001017734

Printed in the United States of America

To

Mister Marvin Knowlen
and
Pastor Jesse Pollmann

for the lessons in drama
and
in the drama of Advent

CONTENTS

PROLOGUE

*C*hristmas plays and pageants have a long and varied history and practice among us. They range from the simplest of skits to the most elaborate of congregational and community undertakings. In some, children costumed from family and church closets walk, and sometimes race, through the lines of Luke 2. In others, choral groups combine with casts of actors and animals to portray the high and holy drama. Perhaps that word explains why plays and pageants continue to beckon congregations large and small, urban and rural, during this season: *drama*. Christmas is, at its heart, dramatic. Movement abounds, backdrops change, action unfolds, scenes change...and a story is enacted by a remarkable cast of characters in an intriguing set of events.

So please note at the beginning: This is not a how-to book to do Christmas plays and pageants. *Setting the Christmas Stage* does explore the characters and settings that comprise the Christmas story. It uses elements from the "stage" to view how Advent gradually pieces together plots, persons, and scenes in order to move the drama to its climax at Christmas.

Why produce this resource rather than another play or script? The rush of activities in Advent, at church and otherwise, can create an obstacle to time spent in reflection on the characters and places that comprise the stories leading to Christmas. Yet the season of Advent means to prepare us for one of the two great festivals of the church, the celebration of Incarnation. This book provides individuals, groups, and churches an opportunity to linger within those stories and their "stagings" of the Christmas drama, that our spirits might encounter more deeply the meaning of God's coming to us in Jesus.

The book derives its structure from Advent and also from a concern for the "busy-ness" of this season. Four chapters correspond to the four weeks in Advent. Each chapter contains four readings; there is not one for each day. The intention here is to allow this book to supplement the season with spiritual reflection, not load it down so that something has to be done every day. The readings explore characters and settings for the Christmas stage that encourage connection between the stories of old to our own spiritual journeys through Advent toward the birth. Take your time as you read these stories. Find the carols suggested for each reading, and listen to them if possible. Let them add another entry into the text and into that day's setting of the stage.

The themes of the book's chapters build upon one another, even as the production of a play requires a methodical construction of set and then characters. "Erecting the Backdrops" will consider how four of Israel's prophets set the context for Advent's drama. "Constructing the Scenery" will view four critical settings where the stories of Advent and Christmas unfold. "Gathering the Choruses" will focus on four groups with special roles in this drama. "Casting the Central Characters" will revisit the four main characters whom we encounter in Christmas. Finally, an epilogue will offer a fictional narrative of the first Christmas, the morning after the birth.

This book is intended for use by those who read it on their own, as part of a small-group study, or as part of some other family or congregational setting. Three appendixes at the end of the book will address concerns related to the resource's use. One appendix will identify the carols linked with each reading and sources where the carols may be found, should you wish to incorporate them into your reflective experience. A second appendix will provide a suggested guide for small-group studies. A third appendix will offer ideas for tying this book to church and/or family Advent celebrations and observances. Even if you are reading on your own, explore the suggested group studies or family/congregational experiences. Perhaps ideas from settings other than your own will enhance your experience with this book.

For those using this book, please notice the biblical text at the top of each reading and the suggested carol at the end. The biblical text gives the scripture reference for that day's reading. Although you may choose to read more from that book as you wish, at *least* read the designated portion. The quote at the top of the reading, beneath the scripture reference, will always be from the selected carol, whose title will be provided at the end as another background "text" for the day's reading.

Again, Advent can become a time when schedules grow hectic and time short. It may seem as if spiritual reflection is an unaffordable luxury. Let this book weigh in against that tendency. Set aside time when you can be with the words (and the music) in quietness and calm. Take what you read here to heart. Wrestle with words of prophets. Envision scenes, though distant, that may seem as close as home this season. Struggle to hear anew the choruses brought by angels and shepherds, magi and martyrs. And watch with parents as words and dreams and birth come to pass...and as God takes the stage in the Child.

Enjoy—and find joy—within these pages and in the drama unfolding on the Christmas stage!

— ACKNOWLEDGMENTS—

*M*any hands have helped set the stage for this book. To draw on distant but powerful memories, Salvator Evangelical and Reformed Church in St. Louis gave me a wealth of Advent and Christmas experiences during my childhood and teenage years. Pastor Jesse Pollmann, in particular, crafted Christmas Eve services that relied on the flow of the story's drama—and gave me a valuable model for drafting such services in my own pastoral ministry.

The good folk at Upper Room Books have, as always, provided support and backing for my pursuit of this project. To JoAnn Miller and Rita Collett, to George Donigian and Sherry Elliott, Sarah Schaller-Linn, Denise Duke, and to numerous others who have worked behind the scenes and made this a better book than its initial draft: I owe you thanks and gratitude for your partnership.

I have read selections of this work to the writers I have been meeting with monthly for over nine years now. They too have shared suggestions and ideas, even as they have offered support and friendship: Pat Thomas, Brian Harrison, Jenelle Varila, Robert Michael Pyle, Sue Holway, and Lorne Wirkkala.

My high school advisor and drama teacher, the late Marvin Knowlen, sparked my interest in theater more than I realized at the time. Perhaps he may now somehow see that "Mr. Indermark" really did gain from his love for literature and the stage. Thanks, M.J.H.K.

Judy Indermark and Jeff Indermark, wife and son to me, provide love and encouragement both gracious in the giving and sustaining in the receiving. The writing life would not go well without them.

WEEK ONE

Erecting the Backdrops

In the theater, backdrops define the height, width, and depth of the stage. They provide the context in which the scenery, characters, and action are all set.

In Advent the prophets of Israel form the backdrops for the stage upon which this season unfolds. Their words of promise and anticipation create the environment within which Advent's drama will take form, shape, and character.

Clearly not every prophetic utterance that flows into the stream of Advent finds consideration here nor does every prophet who spoke a word that the church has subsequently heard as sign of the One who comes. So consider these four singled out for reflection as representative of all the voices crying out for hope in wilderness settings, for light in shadowed places. And let their words help you frame this stage upon which Advent will unfold.

Day 1

———— ISAIAH ————

A Season of Preparing
ISAIAH 40:1-11

Prepare the way, O Zion, your Christ is drawing near!

*N*orman MacLean's book, *A River Runs through It,* begins with this sentence: "In our family, there was no clear line between religion and fly fishing." Let me offer a seasonal paraphrase that holds true in the small town in which I live, and perhaps in communities (and families) you know. In Naselle, there is no clear line between religion and basketball. I do not say that as one of the perennial naysayers, forcing false choices between academics or athletics. For many years my Sunday morning pulpit voice from early December through February has exhibited effects of my Saturday-night bleacher voice.

So what does basketball have to do with the word and message of Isaiah for setting the Christmas stage? The first time I watched our son play an organized basketball game on Naselle's court, he and his third-grade compatriots looked like whirligigs zipping around on a pond, half dribbling, half carrying the ball, until someone managed to launch a shot that might reach the net—or even the rim—if it had sufficient momentum. I've lost track of the number of games Jeff played between then and the final game of his senior year, not to mention the practices, open gym and backyard hoops, and camps. But countless hours of preparation formed the transition between whirligigs and all-league honors.

In the pastor's column to his parishioners targeted for the beginning of Advent, a colleague of mine once wrote,

> *I recently proposed, playfully, that families commit one-third of the time to religious education and formation they commit to sports. The truth, which our Jewish neighbors have long understood, is that acquiring a faith requires at least as much time and effort as becoming skilled at a sport.*

I had two reactions when I first read Tony's words. The first came in gratitude that he used the word *playfully* along with *proposed*, lest the guilt induced by his insight follow me as a parent all the days of my life. The second surfaced in appreciation for putting his finger on the call to disciplined preparation that marks the season of Advent.

Can you imagine the reaction of a high school coach if a young man or woman arrived at the first day of varsity tryouts and announced that what qualified him or her to make the team was playing at Christmas and Easter? Or that once-a-week practices did not take into consideration the busy lifestyles of people living in the Pacific Northwest (you may fill in the region in which you live)? Now I understand athletic teams and communities of faith do not form exact parallels: We need not compete for seats in the sanctuary or places at the table. But the point is this: What signal do we send to the next generation about faith's priority by the example provided in our participation or by our expectations of their involvement, learning, and growth? Like it or not, religious formation requires preparation and discipline.

Nowhere does the theme of preparation sound more clearly than in Advent, particularly in this text from Isaiah 40. *Prepare the way of the Lord....Make straight in the desert a highway for our God....get up to a high mountain....lift up valleys....make low mountains...* (AP).

In Isaiah's depiction of Israel's release from exile, the keynote is preparation: preparation portrayed in the imagery of road-building; preparation proclaimed in the need for life-turning *metanoia* or repentance; in other words, preparation as the rigorous and demanding work of readying lives to welcome the very presence of God into our midst.

One does not adequately prepare for the coming of Christmas merely by unpacking the attic boxes marked "decorations" in time for the tree and the company, only to be put away again until next December. Advent's preparations initiate ongoing disciplines to make room for the coming of Christ into our lives, our communities, and our churches. We make room for God's holy presence by sweeping out the unholy through the discipline of confession and repentance. We make room for Christ's incarnation among us by remembering that how we treat one another reflects how we treat our Lord.

Such disciplines do not happen automatically. Not many among us enjoy the truth that we are not the parents or spouses or children or workers or church members God fashioned us to be. Not many of us find it easy to love people we would never choose as friends. Yet faith calls us to repentance and love, as it has since Isaiah's time. How do we even begin to be faithful to such a calling? By combining hard work and sheer grace, personal discipline and the Spirit's gift. By living one day at a time as those who recognize ourselves for who we are—and who still trust God to help make us who we might yet be. Faithfulness to Advent's disciplined preparation comes in welcoming the very dwelling of God within us.

But this preparation is by no means all work on our part.

Isaiah's words of preparation close with a more tender and gracious vision of God's action in our midst.

> *He will feed his flock like a shepherd;*
> *He will gather the lambs in his arms;*
> *He will carry them in his bosom;*
> *He will gently lead the mother sheep.* (AP)

When the preparations seem long and demanding, Isaiah reminds us that God also comes in tenderness, as a shepherd who cares for those most vulnerable and in need of care.

For too many in this season of Advent, the future holds little hope or promise. The death of a loved one, estrangement within family, depression, illness: any or all of these issues can conspire to close off life from its possibilities. Before repentance can be sounded, comfort must be given. *Comfort my people, says your God. Speak tenderly to Jerusalem.*

That comfort also bears Advent's word of preparation. It declares that hope is still possible. It affirms that grace still awaits. The gift of comfort can take time to work its way into bereaved and conflicted lives. That God-promised comfort seeks community willing to gather lambs and to lead those in need of direction or willing simply to stand alongside those who cannot yet see beyond the hurt or grief: to offer the embrace of Christ's arms, the touch of Christ's hands, the strength of Christ's shoulders.

As you begin this journey through Advent, how do you prepare to welcome God? The ways are as varied as the needs around you—and within you. You prepare your welcome of God when you exercise welcome toward others. You prepare your welcome of God when you empty your life of the sin that crowds out all that is good and gracious. You prepare your welcome of God when you comfort the afflicted with compassion.

So let me playfully propose that during this Advent season we spend as much time preparing to welcome God as we do playing basketball—or as we do shopping or cooking or fussing around the house or hanging all those lights that somehow got tangled in storage—or however we otherwise expend our time and energies preparing for the holiday. Because maybe then, Advent's preparations will become habit and discipline through the rest of the year as well, and we will be ready for the One whose power feeds flocks and gathers lambs.

FOR FURTHER REFLECTION

- What will you do this day to open yourself to the gift of God's presence?
- What will you do to make that gift more accessible to one other person?

CAROL FOR THE DAY—"Prepare the Way"

Day 2

——— JEREMIAH ———

Promise Keeper
JEREMIAH 33:14-16

Come, thou long-expected Jesus, born to set thy people free.

*A*rguably promise keeping is an increasingly lost art. Or maybe promise keeping has *always* been an underdog in this world's domain. Certainly in the public arena, the keeping of promises runs a distant second to the making of promises. Persons seeking public office too often promise whatever is necessary to gain election, hoping no network will put together at reelection time a collection of sound bites of promises not kept. Worse yet is the cynicism bred in the public by such action. When people raise the issue of an unfulfilled promise, they sometimes receive the following reaction: "Well, what did you expect?" Without expectations promises are devoid of power; those who make them escape accountability; and a vicious cycle is created. Who cares if promises go unaddressed? What did you expect?

The debasing of promises in public life affects the way promises are viewed and held in private life. Historians may well judge that one of the most devastating legacies of the last quarter of the twentieth century has been the cynicism bred at the foundation of most every public institution. "Question authority. Don't trust anyone over thirty. Big government is the enemy of democracy." Remember those slogans? Distrust and suspicion have become the accepted norm, whether of voters for politicians, parents for teachers and administrators, laity for clergy, or congregations for denominations. Distrust generates apathy and a lowering of expectations for those we disdain and for the promises they make.

When we assume that promises will be broken and raise no protest, we contribute to an atmosphere that devalues the bond of our words. A promise is no more and no less than our word, our most fundamental expression of who we are. When our word cannot be trusted, can *we* be trusted?

The days are surely coming. With those five words, Jeremiah erects another backdrop on the stage that will give birth to Christmas. But clarification is in order. "The days are surely coming" utters no prophetic oracle to the unstoppable march of shopping days to the 25th of December when, ready or not, the holiday is here. That march of days can drain rather than empower us for the festival at its end. "The days are surely coming" points instead to the time when God's promises will be kept. Christmas is both sign and foretaste of that keeping. It declares that the future ultimately belongs to the realm of God.

Jeremiah confidently promises that "the days are surely coming." But what kind of days will they be? Jeremiah offers a fundamental word about the future by declaring a fundamental word about the God in whose hands the future rests: "The days are surely coming,...*when I will fulfill the promise* I made to the house of Israel and the house of Judah." Jeremiah reveals that the God whose coming we await is, first and foremost, the keeper of promises: Someone whose word will be kept, someone whose word can be trusted.

"The days are surely coming when *I will fulfill the promise* I made." In days of promise breaking or in the equally devastating ignoring of promises as if they do not matter, the declaration of belief in one who keeps promises is an extraordinary act of faith. When Jeremiah first uttered these words to Jerusalem and Judea, the ones entrusted with the care of the people were found to be utterly lacking in the keeping of their vows. Jeremiah elsewhere laments the twisted words of prophets and priests as well as the resulting perversion of expectations: "The prophets prophesy falsely, and the priests rule as the prophets direct; my people love to have it so" (Jer. 5:31). Jeremiah pronounces a similar judgment on the kings of Judea who have distorted their calling to shepherd (literally, "feed") the people into an opportunity to feed upon them.

So when God declares through Jeremiah that God will be the One who will *fulfill* promises, that word comes couched in the language of government and societal order. "I will cause a righteous Branch to spring up for David; and he shall execute justice and righteousness in the land....Judah will be saved and Jerusalem will live in safety." The promises God will keep have to do with matters of fairness and equity. Where the previous "branches" of David's line have faltered, God promises a new branch to take up the cause of justice once more. The future will be different, Jeremiah declares—and we hope—because it will be a place and time of God's promise keeping.

In Advent we perceive Jeremiah's promise through the prism of the manger. David's righteous branch forms an ancient light passed through the birth in Bethlehem, David's own city—and through Joseph, a descendant of Israel's famed king. So we see in Christmas one part of the promise unfolding...but not all of it, not entirely. Those days of which Jeremiah spoke did not fully come in Bethlehem or even upon Calvary. We still long for the promised fulfillment of justice and righteousness in the land. We still yearn to live in places of safety. Those days are surely coming, says the Lord, the Promise Keeper. Advent asks, How do we await them?

Does Advent christen us as those who take a wait-and-see attitude, sitting back while we passively observe the signs of the times? I think not. To proclaim God as the keeper of promises involves us in the unfolding and fulfilling of those same promises. It is not enough to say we long for God's day of justice and equity while exhibiting indifference to cries for justice and fairness among us. It is not enough to say we yearn for God's promise of safety and salvation while remaining unmoved by those for whom sanctuary is literally a matter of life and death.

How we understand and name God intends to transform the conduct of our lives. Advent prepares us for the God who keeps promises by *having us become* keepers of those same promises. Their fulfillment may stretch beyond our effort and our day. Every generation of the faithful has worked and labored to evidence the signs of God's kingdom and rule in their lives and the life of this world—and they have done so without history's drawing to a close or the promises being exhausted. But that in no way excuses inaction on our part, for the Christ who comes, in the words of Paul in Second Corinthians, is the yes to every one of God's promises.

"The days are surely coming [says the Lord] when I will fulfill the promises." So Jeremiah helps set the Christmas stage. Advent wants to know: Do we believe Jeremiah's words? If we do, our lives will not only wait upon those promises with hope, we will act upon those promises with courage. With Jeremiah our faith confesses God as the One who keeps promises. Because of that belief, we may look with confidence to the days that are coming. By our very words and acts of faith, we may begin to live *today* in the light of those days—and in the light of the One whom we may trust to keep what has been promised.

FOR FURTHER REFLECTION

- What promise of God, associated with this season, draws you to prayer and action on its behalf?

- In what ways will you make that promise and its keeping a discipline of your Advent watch?

CAROL FOR THE DAY—"Come, Thou Long-Expected Jesus"

Day 3

——— MICAH ———

When Peace Comes from the West Bank
MICAH 5:2-5A

When peace shall over all the earth its ancient splendors fling...

The most familiar association of Micah with Advent comes in its geographical reference: "But you, O Bethlehem of Ephrathah, who are one of the little clans of Judah, from you shall come forth for me one who is to rule in Israel." Micah's concern, however, reaches far beyond a mere geographical previewing of the Christ's birth, whose fulfillment can be seen as accomplished once and for all. Instead Micah raises the stakes of the Messiah's advent. He transforms the easily recognizable fulfillment in Bethlehem into a vastly different and far less evident sign of the circumstances of God's coming. Listen to Micah's closing word about Bethlehem's promised one: "and he shall be the one of peace."

Micah sets the Christmas stage by adding backdrops that join the *location* of Messiah's birth to the *result* of Messiah's birth. And that promised *result* is peace. The Hebrew word used by Micah is *shalom*. *Shalom* meant far more than an absence of war or conflict. To the prophets, *shalom* signified both fullness and security in life; fear and want are extinguished. How shall we recognize the God who comes, the God for whom we prepare in Advent? Micah announces, "He shall be the one of *shalom*, of peace."

Peace. Peace does not roll off the tongues of Israel's

prophets with the greatest of ease. We find this affirmation in Micah and in Isaiah's landmark identification of God's promised one as the "Prince of Peace." But far more often do the prophets sound condemnation of those who try to paper over deep crises of spirit and nation with claims of "peace."

Thus Ezekiel calls down judgment on those who "have misled my people, saying, 'Peace,' when there is no peace" (13:10). Jeremiah laments the fact that those who should have been truth telling for the sake of renewal have instead "treated the wound of my people carelessly, saying, 'Peace, peace,' when there is no peace" (6:14). Even Micah is no naive idealist, blinded by fervor for peace to its misuse by those who utter its promise for their own end: "Thus says the Lord concerning the prophets who lead my people astray, who cry 'peace' when they have something to eat, but declare war against those who put nothing into their mouths" (3:5).

The prophets' ambiguity on peace arises not because peace is something unimportant or secondary, but because peace stands at the very heart of their expectations. The danger they perceive resides in a willingness to accept poor substitutes and partisan visions of it. In the prophets' times, the country could not secure God's *shalom* by accepting the party plank of the royalists or by entering the latest defense pact with the Egyptians against the Babylonians. Amos, Jeremiah, and others found themselves labeled traitors and enemies of Israel and Judah for speaking a contradictory word to the day's conventional wisdom on where and in whom peace was to be found.

God's *shalom* stretched too broadly to be contained by partisan nationalism. Micah's earlier vision of the coming of God's *shalom* did not restrict itself to a narrow strip of land confined between the Mediterranean Sea and the Jordan River. "Nation shall not lift up sword against nation, neither shall they learn war any more; but they shall all sit under their own vines and under their own fig trees, and no one shall make them afraid"

(4:3-4). Micah insists we remember that "[God] shall be the one of peace."

As disciples eager to point to the historical fulfillment of Micah's *geographical* promise of Bethlehem, we ought also to be disciples who trust in and work toward the historical fulfillment of Micah's promise of *peace*. Christmas should make Christians the most committed group of all peace seekers on earth. Why? If we believe what we say we do, we are the ones who see peace not as fleeting hope but as creation's ultimate destiny. The path of peace resides in our belief that we can trust our lives to God's promises. For if Micah is right, Christmas is not just what happened in a little town called Bethlehem two thousand years ago. Christmas is about the unfolding of a promise whose fulfillment awaits God's realm of *shalom*.

This promise, to be sure, has a long way to go. And Bethlehem, now as then, remains a powerful symbol of how long and elusive the way is. In Micah's time, the reference to Bethlehem would have seemed unlikely. Bethlehem had been David's town, and David's descendants had proved unworthy stewards of the throne, unable to secure Israel's *shalom*. In Jesus' time, the reference to Bethlehem must have seemed ludicrous. Bethlehem had been reduced to an insignificant suburb of Jerusalem. Surely God's peace would have to come through Jerusalem's Herodian palace or its Roman garrison called the Antonia, not some wide spot in the road where no one of any importance came from any more.

In our time, the reference linking Bethlehem with peace still seems untenable. Situated squarely in that region known as the West Bank, Bethlehem is an Arab town with uniformed shepherds watching o'er their flocks by night—and by day—with Uzis. Since the death of Yitzhak Rabin, hope for *shalom* in Micah's promised village remains a tenuous dream. Peace on the West Bank? You've got to be kidding. Bethlehem would be the last place you'd look, as it always has been. But for God, it was the first place. *From you, O Bethlehem...shall be the one of peace.*

The bottom-line trust evoked by Micah's text is this: God *will* bring peace. Some may hear that as letting the church off the hook. "Well, if God will do it, it'll happen when God is good and ready. Nothing we do or say really matters anyway." That might be true, except for one small problem: Christmas. When God decided to act in the fullness of time for redemption, God did not send down an announcement written on stone or paper. God did not stand aloof in the heavens, raining hellfire and damnation down on the heads of sinners. God acted and came in human form. In Bethlehem.

And if God chooses to fulfill promises by an incarnate Messiah, who is to say God will not bring the promised peace, not by manipulating history at a distance but by acting today through persons and institutions of faith? "God will do it, so I don't have to" is a precarious attitude to take with the God of Jesus, the God of incarnate love and grace...and peace.

When the day of God's *shalom* does dawn, may it be said that the Child of Bethlehem, the Prince of Peace, was alive and well in our *shalom*-bringing, peace-making lives—even on the West Bank, even in all the other places where peace remains far more promise than fulfillment. For there, God's *shalom* awaits our trust, our hope, and our making of peace with one another as God has made peace with us in Jesus Christ.

FOR FURTHER REFLECTION

- How do you experience the need for peace in your community, in your church, in your family, in your heart?
- Prayerfully consider how you may seek that peace in these places this season.

CAROL FOR THE DAY—"It Came upon the Midnight Clear"

$\mathcal{D}ay$ 4

—— MALACHI ——

Messengers

MALACHI 3:1-3

Watchman, tell us of the night, what its signs of promise are.

Some of the most entertaining and off-the-wall writing in newspapers appears in the letters to the editor. Some years ago at the beginning of Advent, one of the more creative letters to the editor I've seen in our local weekly compared waiting for the benefits of "trickle down" economics with waiting for the second coming of Christ. Both, the writer concluded, were occurrences on which he would not bet the grocery money.

While some might wish to mold Advent into an extended Christmas, with fulfillment guaranteed every December 25th, Advent's message looms far larger. God's Advent includes (besides a mangered child) the end of history and the establishment of God's realm, or, as the letter to the editor put it, the second coming of Jesus. However we speak of it, Advent stands vigil for God's final coming. That is the message. And every message needs a messenger. Malachi sets the Christmas stage as he anticipates God's provision of such a figure: "See, I am sending my messenger." God's advent does not occur unheralded. The messenger will cry out, not with a timetable but with calls for preparation. Malachi's messenger hangs above the Christmas stage like a hand pointing to the future.

A word of caution here about messengers: In the days of

Malachi, some twenty-five hundred years ago, the role of a messenger could be extraordinarily precarious, especially a messenger to the king. If the news brought to court announced some welcome tidings, the messenger might well be rewarded on the spot. On the other hand, let the messenger bring news of a battle lost or some other tragic event, then woe to the bearer of bad tidings. The ancient world knows no scarcity of stories of messengers struck down simply because they announced bad news.

We are much more civilized today, of course. We do not victimize messengers any more. We simply make them scapegoats. Journalists who do not withhold the bitter statistics of war, poverty, crime, or racism, especially when such things fall too close to home, are blamed for the news itself. Perhaps we believe such things would not exist if we didn't acknowledge them. "Hear no evil, see no evil, then there be no evil" forms the spirit of such contemporary know-nothingism.

So when we hear Malachi pronouncing God's promise that "I am sending my messenger to prepare the way before me," we ought not scratch our heads in wonder at why people didn't automatically redirect their lives. Messengers of news, much less change, are not always welcome, particularly by those who prefer things as they are and always have been, thank you; particularly by those who stand to lose some power or privilege by a reshuffling of the societal deck.

Malachi continues, "Indeed, [my messenger] is coming…but who can endure the day of his coming, and who can stand when he appears? For he is like a refiner's fire and like fullers' soap." Texts like these help us understand why we prefer that Advent focus exclusively on the tender scene of a child cradled in Madonna's arms. Readying ourselves for a birth observed in candlelit wonder is a far cry from preparing ourselves for a rebirth involving a refiner's fiery repentance. Yet Advent's message holds both images together.

The New Testament herald associated with this prophecy seems every bit as raw and powerful as Malachi's expectation. All four Gospels agree on the promised messenger to be the rough-edged person known as John the Baptizer. If anything, Malachi *underestimated* this messenger's stark and controversial nature. Consider Luke's introduction to the long expected messenger. As with the opening of his Christmas story, Luke introduces John by providing a list of all that day's VIPs.

> *In the fifteenth year of the reign of Emperor Tiberius, when Pontius Pilate was governor of Judea, and Herod was ruler of Galilee, and his brother Philip ruler of the region of Ituraea and Trachonitis, and Lysanias ruler of Abilene, during the high priesthood of Annas and Caiaphas...*

After acknowledging all these terribly important people in all their terribly important places and positions, to whom does Luke say God's messenger will come? "The word of God came to John son of Zechariah, in the wilderness." The word comes to...well, a nobody, whose father was a minor temple official never heard from again. Go figure.

Perhaps even more baffling was where the message and messenger of God's Advent could be found: in the wilderness, in a place so out of the way no one could accidentally stumble upon it. The messenger, like the coming he announced, had to be sought deliberately. And even upon finding the messenger known as John the Baptizer, the seeker's work had only just begun, for John's message burned like Malachi's refining fire. To the crowds who made the strenuous journey to hear him, he proclaimed, "Bear fruits worthy of repentance." Talking change in life did not suffice. To those who took pride in spiritual pedigree, he chided, "God is able from these stones to raise up children to Abraham. Even now the ax is lying at the root of the trees." John was not the sort of messenger you'd want to have around your church during stewardship week.

God's Advent demanded core changes in the conduct of life. When the crowds asked John what they should do, his response anticipated a later sermon by the Christ whose way he came to prepare, "Whoever has two coats must share with anyone who has none; and whoever has food must do likewise." When tax collectors came for baptism, they received this instruction: "Collect no more than the amount prescribed for you"; that is, give up your means to make a windfall profit. And soldiers who risked their position by coming to John found the going just as costly: "Do not extort money from anyone...and be satisfied with your wages." Across the board, the message held constant: God's coming meant that business-as-usual was a thing of the past.

That was then, but how is it now? How does the Baptizer's ministry address our Advent preparations? In John, the messenger of God's Advent *then* came in a most unlikely person. So let us not be surprised if the messengers of God's Advent among us are not the highly visible, duly advertised spokespersons of God and society in our midst. If we want to see signs of God's coming among us, perhaps the persons to seek out are those whose lives quietly but profoundly reveal the fruits of repentance announced by John: fruits of sharing from abundance, fruits of practicing vocations in ethical ways, fruits of translating Sunday words into weekday works.

And John, the messenger of God's Advent *then,* came in a most unlikely *place:* the wilderness. So let us not be surprised if God's Advent word continues to be heralded in out-of-the-way locales: soup kitchens, drug rehabilitation centers, halfway homes, in churches and institutions routinely overlooked and underestimated by everyone save the God who works life-changing activity there. Activity that in itself and in the spirit in which it is given announces that God's coming into human life is more than just wishful thinking. It is a summons to service.

"See, I am sending my messenger to prepare the way before me, and the Lord whom you seek will suddenly come." Do you really believe that? Do you really believe in God's Advent and in its demanding preparations? If you do, you will not just want to bet the groceries on God's coming. Your life will be changed: subject to the refiner's fire of Malachi, subject to the call to repentance of the Baptizer, that you and I may be readied for the God who comes.

FOR FURTHER REFLECTION

- Where and from whom do you hear the message of God's coming most poignantly and powerfully declared?
- How is your life different as a result?

CAROL FOR THE DAY—"Watchman, Tell Us of the Night"

WEEK TWO

Constructing the Scenery

In the theater, scenery provides visual clues for the primary settings of unfolding stories and plots. While the stage and play remain the same, changing scenery portrays movement in place, time, and characters.

The scenes of Advent come in a diverse series of places, whose only apparent unity is the approaching birth to which they all are bound: the sitting room of Elizabeth, where she receives a visit from her young cousin Mary; the inn of Bethlehem, where hospitality is tested; the stable, where a barn becomes a birthing ward; the palace of Herod, where power brooks no rivals no matter the cost.

These four places do not exhaust every possible scene for Advent's unfolding. But they do reveal key moments and pivotal choices in its story. So let these scenes take form and shape in your mind's and spirit's eye, that these places of old may shed light on the places in which you and I live our lives and greet Advent's coming into our midst.

$\mathcal{D}ay$ 1

—— ELIZABETH ——

A Sitting Room
LUKE 1:24-25, 39-45, 56-57

People, look east and sing today. Love, the Guest, is on the way.

A sitting room. Do you have one in your house—a room devoted to the purpose of, well, sitting? In some homes the living room comes closest to this, although televisions, multimedia entertainment centers, and computer consoles linked to the Internet make these rooms far too active and "busy" to consider them sitting rooms. Sitting rooms make it possible and encourage silence to be kept, conversations to be heard, and waiting to be patiently, if not at times excruciatingly, observed.

The opening scene to the Christmas stage occurs in just such a room. Or, since first-century Palestinian homes were often single-room dwellings with areas devoted to various uses, it would at least represent such an area. One chair, or two. A window that looks out on some vista inviting the occasional gaze. Or perhaps a painting whose view affords the one who sits an opportunity to study the shapes and colors and see things not seen before. It would be the sort of place where

Elizabeth, and later her cousin, Mary, could engage solitude as well as dialogue and where hopes and joys might be given a quiet womb in which to grow and mature.

"After those days [Zechariah's] wife Elizabeth conceived, and for five months she remained in seclusion" (Luke 1:24). For Elizabeth the need of a sitting room likely presented itself initially as an escape from the outside world. Years and decades of bearing the scorn of one who was barren would not quickly dissipate, even with the life growing within her. The sneers and smirks of those who ridiculed her before might not find their silencing now, perhaps only a new occasion for the exercise of gossip. After all, having a priest-husband muted did not necessarily signal God's favor. Who's to say others would not attribute the swelling of the child within her to a combination of wishful thinking and overeating? The seclusion of five months evokes the image of a retreat into solitude, into safety, into sanctuary. Christmas's birthing begins where no prying eyes or wagging tongues can harm, where God's power can work in the grace of stillness.

But stillness need not mean isolation. Solitude need not come without community. And to the props of this sitting room, a second chair comes into play. "In those days Mary set out and went with haste to a Judean town in the hill country, where she entered the house of Zechariah and greeted Elizabeth" (Luke 1:39-40). Now the scene becomes more familiar, bringing onstage a character with whom we are much acquainted. Still, this is not the scene of Mary receiving the angelic visit to disclose what will be asked of her. This is not the scene of Mary cradling the child beside a manger, wondering at shepherds' words. In this scene Mary greets her cousin Elizabeth, who breaks a five-month seclusion with what will become a three-month shared vigil (Luke 1:56). In this sitting room, two women sit, speak, listen…and wait for the promised life within each to grow, develop, and mature.

This scene might seem an unusual one with which to open the Christmas staging. Perhaps something a little flashier, a little louder, a little catchier might be in order. After all, this is the promised birth of the Messiah, the Only Begotten of the Holy One of Israel. Maybe a couple of digital billboards in the background and low-rumbling subwoofers pounding out the bass and beat of "Joy to the World" would catch more attention, turn more heads, and startle more eyes.

However, Advent does not seize our senses without consent. The premise of its new birth is such that we have to search out its signs to become aware of new life and fresh hope.

In Elizabeth's sitting room, the leaping of the child within her is about as wild as the action gets. To sense such movement requires quiet and stillness, for attention must be paid not to the clamor without but to the life within. Advent and the coming Christmas joy are not first perceived in the unmistakable shaking of the world's foundations but in the pirouette of a prophet in utero.

From such hidden stirrings Elizabeth pronounces blessing upon the guest who has come and the one Mary bears within her. Repeating words bestowed previously in the Hebrew Scriptures upon the likes of Jael and Judith, Elizabeth declares Mary blessed among women. Her blessing of the fruit within Mary's womb likewise recalls Moses' blessing upon Israel (Deut. 28:4). Such blessings, derived from the old scrolls, reveal that her young cousin stands in a long tradition of figures reckoned blessed by God. But unlike Jael and Judith, Mary's blessedness comes, not joined to slashing of swords (Judg. 5:24; Judith 13:18), but from something far more subtle—yet far more powerful. "Blessed is she who believed that there would be a fulfillment of what was spoken to her by the Lord" (Luke 1:45). In the quietness of the sitting room, Elizabeth comes to understand and declare that Mary's trust in God's purposes is what sets her apart for such honor.

Linking trust to Advent bears remembrance in our day, no less than Mary's. Too often what drives the spirit of this season is not trust in the unseen purposes of God but the mere passage of days to a sure and certain end on December 25. It is not unusual to find persons and families worn down by the march of Advent's days. With so much to do and with increasingly little time in which to do it, we rush and scurry as though it all depended upon us—whether we define the "all" as the holiday dinner or the family reunion or the tree stocked full to overflowing.

Have you ever felt winded by the time it was all over? Have you ever felt as if days and events have come and gone in such a rush that somehow, somewhere, Christmas got misplaced, if not lost, in all the commotion?

If so, consider taking time to enter and to dwell within this first scene. Enter this sitting room where Elizabeth and Mary sit and visit and wait. Dwell in this place where time stands still for the sake of reflecting upon the birth that is to come. Enter this womb where quietness invites us to be still and listen, feeling in the movement of an unborn child within its mother the slowly growing joy that gradually matures, taking its own precious and needed time to reach a birthing.

Elizabeth remained five months in seclusion. Then Mary stayed three months with Elizabeth. What time can you spend in quietness this season, in solitude kept and shared? Advent comes not only in the rush of angels' wings but in the hush of spirits becalmed in trust and hope.

Blessed are those who believe in the fulfillment that comes quite apart from our sometimes anxious efforts and exhausting busyness: a fulfillment that traces to the handiwork of God moving unseen and at a seeming snail's pace; a fulfillment recognized and readied by those whose preparations grow out of the waiting, listening, and trusting of a sitting room.

- How will you fashion times and places of quietness this Advent and beyond for prayer, for waiting, for developing a trusting spirit?

- What new signs of life do you feel stirring inside you this Advent?

Carol for the Day—"People, Look East"

Day 2

── INNKEEPER ──

A Crowded Inn
Luke 2:7b

In the bleak midwinter a stable place sufficed...

Here's a trivia question you can use this season: Who was the first villain of Christmas? To some weaned on the writings of the late Dr. Seuss, the infamous Grinch who stole Christmas might be the reply. To others oriented to earlier literary classics, Charles Dickens's character of Scrooge might be suggested. Certainly King Herod deserves nomination; we will take up his story later in this week. But even Herod was not the first villain. That rather dubious honor belongs to someone whom the Gospels fail to mention, save in the oft-quoted consequence of his action: "There was no room for them in the inn" (KJV). From that single phrase in one Gospel has arisen centuries-old contempt for Bethlehem's innkeeper, the first villain of Christmas: the one who made outcasts of Joseph and Mary at the time when she was to deliver her firstborn; the one who insured Jesus' birthing occurred in a place fit for animals, not infants. Why? *Because there was no room.*

So how might we rightly picture this scene for the Christmas stage? A crowded hotel lobby with a "no vacancy" sign blazing its neon unwelcome through the window into the night? Or, perhaps more in keeping with the realities of a first-century caravansary: a dining room with tables pushed to the edges, its earthen floor now crisscrossed with bodies wrapped in blankets and sheepskins, a snore here, a yawn there, and a rough-hewn 2 x 4 drawn through a pair of brackets to secure the door against any comers? Or might we even envision the childhood game of musical chairs, where the number of participants always outnumbers the available chairs and where the ceasing of the music always means that someone is left without a place? However we envision the scene, its core dilemma remains the same: no room in the inn. And the villainy of Christmas comes attached to the one who made that assessment and conveyed its news to Mary and Joseph.

Some interpreters have wondered about exactly what sort of place turned down the couple. After all, the story does seem to cut against the grain of typical assumptions made about Middle Eastern hospitality. One possibility about the "lodgings" (another way to translate the Greek word usually rendered as "inn") would be a private home, especially one belonging to a relative of Joseph. If that were the case, however, it would have been natural for Luke to make that identification as part of documenting Joseph's Davidic lineage and linkage to this town.

The other suggestion for "lodgings" is the more traditional translation of "inn." Keep in mind, though, that the inns of first-century Palestine were not quaint bed-and-breakfasts possessing private rooms with a view and a fluffy comforter turned down by a proprietor eager to pamper your every whim. Caravansaries squeezed dining, sleeping, and stable space to maximize the profit to be gained from hosting overland traders, merchants, and their stock—and sometimes pilgrims. The abundance of limestone caves in the region around Bethlehem plays well into the tradition that the stable finally found for birthing had been built in a cave.

So we cannot conclusively identify where or what this "inn" was in Bethlehem. That part of the scene remains slightly out of focus. But what comes into clear sight and sharp view is its consequence: "there was *no room* for them."

No room. Forget for a moment about what this scene *looked* like. We have the crucial detail of what it *felt* like: no room. Have you ever experienced that sensation of having no room, no place to be? Worse yet, have you experienced the rejection of being told you do not belong, you do not fit in? That experience also belongs to this story. Perhaps if Joseph had flashed a bit more coin to catch the innkeeper's attention or dropped a few locally renowned names to sway the innkeeper's decision, the scene would have differed. Sometimes the judgment of "no room" has less to do with "no space for anyone" and everything to do with "no chance for the likes of you."

Something of that spirit from this story is kept alive in Christmas pageants that seek to retell the Christmas story in contemporary settings. There, Joseph and Mary are the homeless couple whose car breaks down and who don't have enough cash for the local Motel 6. Or the holy couple appear as dark-skinned in a light-skinned neighborhood or vice-versa. In those pageants the tension arises over whether those to whom they turn for help will be overwhelmed with human compassion—or whether, again, there will be no room for the likes of them, a judgment solemnly intoned by those who would serve as our day's innkeepers—or gatekeepers.

In one of his Christmas sermons, Martin Luther offered an intriguing lesson from this scene of "no room at the inn":

Shame on you, wretched Bethlehem! The inn ought to have been burned with brimstone, for even though Mary had been a beggar maid or unwed, anybody at such a time should have been glad to give her a hand.

There are many of you in this congregation who think to yourselves: "If only I had been there! How quick I would have been to help the Baby! I would have washed his linen.

How happy I would have been to go with the shepherds to see the Lord lying in a manger!" Yes, you would! You say that because you know how great Christ is, but if you had been there at that time you would have done no better than the people of Bethlehem....Why don't you do it now? You have Christ in your neighbor.

Christ in your neighbor: even in the ones cast out into the night, even in the ones for whom we have no room among us. Making room for others is not just a matter of finding unused space, as may have been the problem in Bethlehem. Making room for others may require adjustment to our schedules, or to our thinking, or—God forbid—to the way we do things around here, however you define here. Family, congregation, community, it doesn't matter: making room can be hard work. Too hard often for persons and institutions ingrained in habits and for circles grown immovably comfortable from not being stretched of late.

Why don't you do it now? You have Christ in your neighbor. The stage of Christmas can sometimes wax sentimental, its story so familiar we entrap all its details in the devotion of a long-past scene. But I think Luther has it exactly right when it comes to "no room." The Christmas stage is not a once-upon-a-time recitation: It is where we continue to live our lives and make our choices...and, yes, decide who we will make room for in our lives. Or not.

I suspect the innkeeper of old possibly may have acted entirely innocently in turning Joseph and Mary away. Rooms filled, floor covered: He was just passing on the fact of the matter. But sometimes facts do not cut it. It is not enough to say how things are and close the door. Sometimes, when need presents itself, things must get changed. People need to get moved so another can have room. Space needs to be made, so the Christ can wiggle into the tightness of our lives and schedules and busyness and remind us that the season of Advent is not about closing doors but opening hearts to the God who comes in strangers seeking shelter—and in a sovereign realm where how we make room for the least among us reveals how we make room for God. So we learn at the scene of the inn.

FOR FURTHER REFLECTION

- Who might benefit from your making room for them in your life?
- What changes will making that room require of you?

CAROL FOR THE DAY—"In the Bleak Midwinter"

Day 3

——— ANIMALS ———

A Stable

LUKE 2:12

*And the friendly beasts around him stood, Jesus,
our brother, strong and good.*

I have vague memories of visiting relatives in Nebraska as a young child, relatives who owned and worked on a farm. I don't recall anything our city-bred family did there in particular, but I do remember a barn where the aromas of rough wood, straw floors, leather harnesses, and fresh manure all mingled in summer's heat to produce the sickeningly sweet smell of that place. Some say that scents provide the strongest and most vivid of our memories. I tend to agree. Decades later, two thousand miles distant, I encountered those same aromas in dairy farms and barns on the floodplains of the Grays and Snoqualmie Rivers. Those places transport me back to a landlocked farm in Nebraska and a barn that has likely been reduced to the paneling in the den of some Omaha seeker of things rustic. But I can almost guarantee that den does not carry the full smell of the barn with it. We prefer things to *look* rustic, not *smell* it.

I have never been to a Christmas pageant yet where the stage emanated odors of the original setting of the story. Keep that in mind, heart, and nostril as we prepare to set the next scene for the Christmas stage: the stable. Here a *manger* (a five-dollar word for a feeding trough) once served as crib for the Word Incarnate. Here the animals that normally would have fed out of that trough now had to wait their turn. Here the Only Begotten of God was birthed in a barn, or at least Bethlehem's equivalent of one.

There has been some dispute over the centuries concerning the exact setting of Jesus' birth. The church historian Roland Bainton notes that the artwork of the Western church tends to place Jesus' birth in a shed, while the Eastern church favors a cave or grotto *(Behold the Christ*, 40). The apocryphal work known as the *Protevangelium* asserts that Joseph and Mary found a cave outside Bethlehem in which the birth took place. Visitors to the Church of the Nativity in Bethlehem may view a candlelit grotto, which tradition holds as the birthplace.

And Luke? The only detail as to this place comes in the mention of the "manger." Curiously, Luke makes a major point of the manger. He mentions it not once, not twice, but three times (2:7, 12, 16) in his account of the Christmas story. So whether we picture this scene set beneath the wooden rafters of a shed or the jagged ceiling of a cave, central to the props will be the manger—the feeding trough. And where there is feed, there will be animals.

To generations weaned on crèche sets and carols ("the cattle are lowing, the baby awakes"), the presence of animals in this scene is not surprising. Indeed, it would be unnatural to conceive of a stable or manger without them, especially if the inn were so full. Not only would the stable (or cave) shelter the resident collection of sheep, goats, and draft animals, it would provide lodging for the beasts of burden that brought the pilgrims and traders to town. In my own envisioning of this scene, Joseph would have been busied not only tending to Mary but keeping track of the animals that crowded the stable as much as their owners crowded the inn...

Joseph had carpentered in stables before, patching roofs, adding stalls, repairing yokes. In those times, he relied on the owner to clean up after the animals and see to their keeping. But now, with Mary and the newborn to think of, it fell to him to keep the stable a fit place for mother and child. Oddly, Joseph constantly found it necessary to shoo the animals from the manger, herding them to the corner where their food had been moved. But they kept coming back— the cow's slow loping, the sheep's brisker step, the dove's fluttered swoop— to peer over the manger at the child. Joseph kept reminding himself it must be force of habit. Curiosity is a human emotion. Shepherds could be curious, not cattle or sheep. But for the life of him, the look on the faces of the shepherds last night as they peered over the slats differed little from the faces of cattle and sheep and dove that continued to wander in the child's direction...

Older legends and traditions place even greater emphasis on the presence and roles of the animals. Perhaps the most significant legend attending to the animals goes by the name "The Night of Miracles." According to that legend, the animals kneel at midnight to worship the newborn Jesus. Another version of this legend holds that, at midnight, the stable animals receive the gift of speech. The carol suggested for this scene, "The Friendly Beasts," comes from a medieval French rendering of this legend, where each of the animals in the stable sings of its gift to the Christ Child.

Now I suspect some may begin to wonder at this point how far afoot we have gone from the text of the story, not to mention from reasonable and rational understandings of the scene. Talking animals? Animals that worship? Animals that do not even appear in the Christmas story of Luke? What role *do* animals have to play in this scene of the stable, beyond cardboard props of reclining sheep, lowing cattle, and braying donkeys?

If it were possible, I think shoveling in a load of real barn straw along with a few animals that don't necessarily follow their scripted cues would go a long way toward setting this scene in its proper context. Jesus' birth did not take place in a sterilized birth ward with marble floors gleaming from regular washings with antiseptic soap. The animals may or may not have been talking, but I suspect the silence of the night was not as pristine as sometimes imagined. Christ was born into the world as it is, into our lives as we are. The scene and smell of the stable and its animals remind us of that truth.

More deeply, the stable and its animals remind us that the birth in this place has to do with more than human destiny alone. The whole universe becomes a changed place as a result. Remember that the hymn goes "joy to the *world*": The whole *earth* receives her sovereign and the benefits of God's grace. The hopes of the prophets for God's peaceable realm begin to unfold in the manger. That hope was envisioned long ago in another text that described the dwelling together of wolves and lambs, calves and lions, all led by a little child.

In the stabled manger Isaiah's little child nestles, the feed of animals his cushion and bed. Do the animals really speak, do their knees actually bow down in worship? Of the old legends, who can say? But know that the animals belong to this scene, for they remind us of its earthy reality. They may even point us toward its prophetic hopes of the child who shall lead us all.

For Further Reflection

- How would Christmas be different without the stable and its creatures?
- How will you incorporate the roles of stable and animals into your Advent and Christmas observances?

Carol for the day—"The Friendly Beasts"

Day 4

HEROD

The Palace Throne Room
MATTHEW 2:1-4, 7-8, 16A

Disperse the gloomy clouds of night,
and death's dark shadows put to flight.

*I*n the theatrical world, script writers and playwrights take great time and care in determining when and how to bring a play's characters onstage or into the camera's view. Key characters often will be kept out of sight until some critical juncture when their dramatic entrance portends the role they will have as the production unfolds. At other times, they modestly drift into the ensemble, their importance to the action taking time to emerge and establish.

Matthew sets his Christmas stage in the first verse of our text with a host of characters in plain view: "In the time of King Herod, after Jesus was born in Bethlehem of Judea, wise men from the East came to Jerusalem." Later readings will focus on the Magi and Jesus, leaving us now to face this monarch named Herod in the palace from which he rules. History often adds "the Great" to Herod's name and rightly so. Herod ruled Judea for almost forty years. He counted among his friends and supporters the likes of Mark Antony and Cleopatra and Augustus Caesar. During his reign Herod inaugurated many construction projects to serve as his legacy, the rebuilding of the Jerusalem temple being the most memorable.

But Herod the Great (Builder) could also be just as accurately portrayed as Herod the Great (Butcher). Herod was quick to preside over the death of opponents, regardless of their standing in the community or in his family. The historian Josephus links the king with the murder of several of his sons and at least one wife. So vicious did the king become that even his old friend Augustus coined an amusing, though chilling, play on words to describe Herod. After Herod ordered the execution of two heirs for their alleged part in a plot against him, Augustus supposedly remarked that "It is better to be Herod's pig (hys) than his son (huios)." Remember, that is a friend's description of Herod.

So when the scene of Herod's throne room commandeers the Christmas stage, take care. Herod's palace introduces the stench of death even before the Magi bring word of a newborn king. Herod's greatness traces not to a generous spirit more than willing to extend welcome to any and all claimants to the throne. Herod's greatness stems from years of surviving plot after plot, real and imagined. Herod accepts and practices the fundamental rule of power politics: win at any cost. Hang onto position no matter who pays.

Did you notice the first attitude attributed to Herod in Matthew's text? Fear. When Herod hears the news of a child born king: "*He was frightened.*" The particular word Matthew uses to describe Herod's reaction occurs only one other time in his Gospel. There it describes the reaction of the disciples to the sight of Jesus walking on the stormy waters of Galilee's Sea. Here the storm rages within Herod. An old man finds himself frightened by an infant. As ludicrous as that sounds on the surface, it makes eminent sense for such a one as Herod. Fear will always seek to deny the future in an attempt to hold onto the past, no matter the price.

The story becomes uncomfortably contemporary in its depiction of the degree of deception and eventual brutality to which persons obsessed with power will go to maintain their position. What Herod does here differs little in spirit from a number of episodes in history, ancient and modern. Persons who work for peace in Ireland or the Middle East become targets for those who have a stake in maintaining conflict. Chinese students seek the most tentative of democratic structures, and tanks transform Tiananmen Square from an embryonic Constitution Hall to a modern slaughter of the innocents.

The story, as narrated by Matthew, involves some incongruities. Would Jewish leaders cooperate with the same Herod they hated with a passion for being an outsider and the one who years ago allegedly had ordered the murder of a number of Sanhedrin members, according to Josephus? Would the king not have sent soldiers or spies to follow the Magi to the child, rather than trust they would return on their own? Some argue that the lack of any record of Herod's atrocity against the children of Bethlehem in contemporary sources that detail his other outrages implies this story must be simply a pious myth.

But perhaps other sources pro-Roman in outlook did not view this particular incident as all that notable. A quiet massacre of Jews in an off-the-track village might not have warranted much attention. It is said history is written by the victors, and Herod in his time may well have held the upper hand and (almost) successfully quashed this story.

Beyond such ambiguities, however, the story rings true not just about Herod but about every entrenched holder of power, political and otherwise, who is bound and determined to hold onto such control at any cost. And costs will come. Those costs provide the uneasy undercurrent winding from the throne room in Herod's palace through the cradles in Bethlehem and on through the slaughter of those innocents who still remain tyranny's easiest victims.

It almost seems unfair to ruin the pageant of Christmas by introducing this last of its scenes. Doesn't the world face enough suffering? Don't we have to deal with the harsher sides of reality too many other times? Can't we just have the carols, the candlelight, and the cradles?

Herod spoils Christmas, you know. At least he tries. And maybe that is why this scene becomes inescapable. The likes of Herod recall the contrast brought to us in the reign of the child born in the manger. Jesus' reign brings justice and mercy, not vengeance and brutality. And in the clash between those two reigns, we find our allegiances called to choose whom we will serve once the shepherds have gone home, once the star has set from the sky, once the miracle of Christmas birth turns toward the discipline of Christmas living. Whose realm will we serve in the conduct of our lives and the exercise of our love?

Matthew said that not only was Herod frightened but "all Jerusalem with him." Power based in brutality relies on the contagion of fear. When people acquiesce to fear, the Herods of this world win. But when we insist that fear does not have the final say, when we declare our trust in grace and dare our practice of mercy and compassion, then new birth, new life takes shape. Giving Herod his scene on this stage becomes his undoing. In spite of all the violence, in spite of all the death and grief, by chapter's end Herod dies…and Jesus lives.

The throne room scene reminds us that Christmas is a story about power and in whom the power finally resides. The king is dead. Long live the King!

For Further Reflection

- What fears confront you this season?
- How do the hopes of Advent affect your facing of those fears in practical ways?

Carol for the day—"O Come, O Come, Emmanuel"

WEEK THREE

Gathering the Choruses

"Choruses" today often refer to the refrain sung at the end of each verse of a song or brief "praise songs" used in worship. A slightly older meaning of "chorus" may call to mind the image of a "chorus line" of dancers or perhaps the background singers in a musical production.

The "choruses" for Advent, however, trace back to a far more ancient practice in Greek theater. There individuals sharing some common identity or vocation comprised "choruses" that recited lines in unison that often revealed key elements to the plot or drama. The stage of Advent fills with the sound and presence of four such choruses, each yielding critical insight into the unfolding story: the joyful news of the angels, the boisterous praise of the shepherds, the mysterious revealings of the Magi, the minor-key requiem of the martyred innocents.

Pay close attention to these groups, whose movement on and off the stage indicates changing directions within the Advent drama. Listen to the word they add to that story, in one case through no word left recorded but by utter silence left hanging in the air. From these choruses learn of Advent's emergence into light...and darkness.

Day 1

—— THE ANGELS ——

Announcers
LUKE 2:9-14

Angels we have heard on high, sweetly singing o'er
the plains...Gloria in excelsis Deo

*A*ngels. Church and society tend to go through cycles on how we view these cryptic figures. The last decade or so has been good for angels, at least in terms of commercial appeal and marketability. A spate of books including one by Billy Graham, several television series, a movie where none other than John Travolta dons not a white disco leisure suit but a pair of wings: Angels are in. As the old song once put it, we've grown accustomed to their face.

But have we become as accustomed to their *place?* When all is said and done, angels do not appear (at least in the biblical texts) in order to assure that the world at large and our own individual places of life go on unchanged. In the Bible, visits of angels bring revelations of detours ahead, of major changes impending, of lives and destinies soon to be impacted. Little wonder then that a common initial reaction to the flapping of angel wings in the biblical texts is fear. While fleeing from his brother, Esau, Jacob dreams of a ladder extending into heaven with angels ascending and descending. When he wakes, Genesis 28:17 declares, "[Jacob] was afraid."

We need not retreat that far to perceive the link between the entrance of angels and the onset of fear. Look at Luke's "preamble" to the Christmas story. An angel appears to Zechariah, eventual father of John the Baptizer, bringing news of a son's promised birth. But before a word can be spoken: "When Zechariah saw him, he was terrified; and fear overwhelmed him" (Luke 1:12). When Gabriel comes to Mary to announce the promise of Jesus' birth, "she was much perplexed" (Luke 1:27), a state that resulted in Gabriel's next words to her of "do not be afraid."

Do not be afraid. That also serves as the first word spoken by the angel to shepherds in the field (Luke 2:10) and later by an angel to two women at the tomb (Mark 16:6). When angels appear on the scene, it would seem, fear is not far behind—and for good reason. When angels appear, something of the divine breaks in upon human history, something that exceeds our understanding, not to mention our control; something that pronounces there is more to life than what meets the eye in the keeping of a flock or the maintaining of a career or the "business as usual" sign we hang on our relationships and commitments. When angels descend, fear of the new and the unknown shakes us with the announcement that God is up and about and on the move.

"I am bringing you good news of great joy for all the people: to you is born this day in the city of David a Savior, who is the Messiah, the Lord." The angel who spoke to shepherds in the fields outside Bethlehem seeks to disarm their fears with a word concerning the birth of good news. It is a word that has worldwide implications ("for all the people"), yet a word that bears the most personal of implications ("to you"). The word speaks of Savior, Messiah, and Lord.

The role of the angel as messenger or herald in this story parallels the role played by heralds or messengers in the Roman empire. They brought the news that the emperor wanted to circulate, whether an announcement of military victory or news of a census or word of an heir's birth. More than mere historical detail is at work when Luke opens the Christmas story narrative with the decree that went out from Emperor Augustus. Augustus was a figure revered for his ending of the civil wars that divided Rome and the empire following Julius Caesar's assassination. Grateful citizens erected monuments to celebrate the peace brought by Augustus. An inscription at Halicarnassus hailed him as "savior of the whole world." Another inscription relates that "the birthday of the god [Augustus] has marked the beginning of the good news for the world."

Does all of this sound familiar: peace, savior, good news for the world? It does to those who listen to the announcement of the angel in Luke 2:9-10 and then the refrain of the "multitude of the heavenly host" in verse 14: "Glory to God in the highest heaven, and on earth *peace* among those whom [God] favors!" The angel as messenger announces another Savior, another worldwide realm, another peace that will in time overshadow even the likes of Augustus and Rome.

But not yet. Notice where the first of Advent's choruses sets up shop to announce this world-turning news: out in the fields, in the dark of night, on the hills outside Bethlehem. Had Augustus dispatched messengers across the empire with news of vital importance only to have them limit their pronouncements to practically uninhabited wilderness outside backwater towns at a time when no decent person would be up and about, heads would have rolled. This would be akin today to a presidential address announcing the guarantee of universal peace being broadcast only by a local access cable channel serving the greater Femme de Osage, Missouri, metro area in the hours between the Midnight W.C. Fields Movie Fest and Dawn's Early Light Aerobics.

In Christmas pageants I have seen and in those in which I once took part, the angels usually had a prominent place on stage. One favored roost for the angel declaring "do not be afraid" would be a stepladder or some other location accentuating both height above and centrality to the action. I have grown unsure of the wisdom of such placement. Perhaps the best location for this first Advent chorus, the angels, would be off-stage. They could still be heard, but they would be hard to see. After all, their message remains hard to see; it requires trust.

To be sure, the angelic word about the child wrapped in bands of cloth and lying in a manger points to a vivid image of this season's fulfillment. But what of the announcement of "good news of great joy for *all* the people?" The last time I watched CNN, even on Christmas Eve, not all the people evidenced great joy. People who still live in squalor will not always find great joy in this life. Then again, for people who live with extraordinary wealth at their disposal, having a good time does not guarantee great joy.

The ensuing song sung by the angels presents a more difficult challenge: "Peace among those whom [God] favors." Unless I missed the broadcast on the Femme de Osage channel, peace does not yet reign supreme and unchallenged. And for many folks God's favor does not even seem tenable, much less obvious: not when long-term debilitating illness strikes, not when a child dies violently, not when Alzheimer's slowly but surely strips dignity, mind, and spirit.

So I would place the angel chorus offstage for the time being. Why? Not because their message is wrong or without consequence. Rather, this first of Advent's choruses reminds us that the word brought by angels requires faith on our part. Our hearing it does not depend upon how cute or striking the speaker may be but on our trusting the God-gracing word in the dark when we cannot see everything around and before us, when fears still beset us not only of the dark but of the light.

"To *you* is born this day…." To you, to me, to all: a Savior, who is the Messiah, the Lord. So say the angels. So say you?

FOR FURTHER REFLECTION

- Where, and from whom, do you hear the angels' message of peace and God's favor sounded and enacted today?

- What fears prevent or distract you from receiving that message wholeheartedly?

CAROL FOR THE DAY—"Angels We Have Heard on High"

Day 2

— THE SHEPHERDS —

Movers and Praisers
LUKE 2:15-18, 20

You'll forget your flocks, you'll forget your herds:
rise up, shepherd and follow.

I love crèche sets, scenes of the Nativity. Whether carved in wood or stone, or poured in plastic molds, they have long held a special fascination for me. One of my most cherished Christmas possessions is the Christ child from my grandparents' crèche set, the only surviving piece of it I have. What sort of material it's made from eludes me, rubberized plastic being my best guess. The 25-cent price stamped on the bottom leads me to think it is not some rare malleable ivory. But each Advent, it finds an honored place on the tree or mantel.

I love crèche sets, but I have a problem with them. They are static. No matter how skilled the artisan who fashions the figures, no matter how detailed the looks on the faces or the folds in the robes, the figures in the crèche do not move. During Advent some churches add one or more figures of the crèche to the altar scene each week, giving the impression of change and movement. But even that does not catch the spirit of a mother giving birth or a father busy helping, of wise men following a star or of shepherds racing pell-mell across the fields.

This second chorus of the Advent stage, the shepherds, appears abruptly and with no small commotion. The text speaks first of their fear at the angels' words but then of their haste to discover the truth for themselves. The initial shock of light and voices from the night sky, coupled with the amazing news announced, must have raised their blood pressures. We might picture this tiny band scrambling down rocky hillsides, trying to protect ankles from twists and bodies from falls while at the same time racing to be the first to see if what they had heard were indeed the words of angels—and not the backwash of a bit too much wine to ward off the night's chill. So enter the shepherds upon the scene and into the stable.

But what does it mean to have shepherds come stumbling and stomping into Luke 2? First-century Judaism did not hold shepherds in the same esteem with which we may think of shepherds: fair-haired youth and noble elders whose vocation necessarily embodied self-sacrifice and love for the flock. Jesus' later parable of the good shepherd in John 10 presumes, and even speaks of, the not-so-good shepherd. As we have discovered from rabbinic documents of the day, shepherds as a whole represented an outcast group, not to be trusted because of (alleged) inherent dishonesty. One section of the Babylonian Talmud adds shepherds to the list of those ineligible to be judges or even witnesses in trials. The very practice of their vocation, which required significant times away from community and synagogue, exacerbated their separation from the wider community. Like women, also considered unreliable witnesses at this time but who later served as Easter's first witnesses, so now do shepherds serve as the initial witnesses to the good news of Christmas.

One hallmark of Luke's Gospel involves the bringing to prominence in Jesus' ministry or teaching figures otherwise routinely considered outcasts. That theme finds first light in shepherds hastening to the manger. To those whom decent folk would have been under no obligation to listen to, much less believe, God entrusts the announcement of new birth and new hope. Like good Samaritans and a loving father of both the prodigal and the resentful sons, the shepherds come to the manger as sign and token that the cast of characters parading to and from this child during his life will not always be the ones we might expect. They will not always be the ones bearing the Pharisaic stamp of approval in their time or our own. God's choice of shepherds to hear the news and make the first pilgrimage brings to the Christmas stage the word that the only stamp of approval of consequence in this child's life and ministry will be that of God's grace.

The shepherds provide other insights into God's recreation now squirming in the straw in Bethlehem's manger. Shepherd had been an early image for the kings of Israel. And the kings of Israel had been a bitter disappointment ever since Samuel first warned the Israelites against their desire to have a king "like other nations." The old prophet railed against the way kings would take the sons and daughters of the people and press them into their service; he cautioned them against monarchs who would seize the best land and crops and give it to their own lackeys (1 Sam. 8:4-22). Yet the Israelites insisted, and the classic warning about being careful what we ask for lest we get it came upon them in the person of Saul.

The great disappointment with the kings came to a head with the onset of exile. Recall how the prophet Ezekiel understood the word of God's judgment in those days: "Prophesy against the *shepherds* of Israel….Should not shepherds feed the sheep?…You have not strengthened the weak, you have not healed the sick" (Ezek. 34:2, 4). The entire first half of Ezekiel 34 indicts the shepherds for failing to care for the people, and the remaining half of the chapter announces God's promise to care for the scattered sheep of Israel. Indeed, Ezekiel's vision of restoration involves one shepherd: "I will set up over them one shepherd, my servant David, and he shall feed them: he shall feed them and be their shepherd" (34:23).

Shepherds now gathered on the Christmas stage bring that promise into remembrance. They do so even more powerfully than we might imagine, for do we remember David's vocation as a young man before joining the armies of Israel to stand before Goliath? Shepherd. David shepherded on the hillsides of Bethlehem long before he knew the halls of power in Jerusalem. From those same hillsides, shepherds now come in a mad downhill rush to see the one born in the city of David, one of their own. They come to see a child who was born, like their own children, in poverty and obscurity; a child who finds his life, as they find theirs, among sheep and lambs. Yet this child provides the answer to the promised words of *Savior* and *Messiah* and *Lord*, all three titles suggesting the sort of power once associated with David.

"Glory to God in the highest." If, as Luke 2:17 suggests, the shepherds made known to Mary and Joseph what had been told them, then they included this portion of the angel's song in the report. It will be a word not heard again on the stage of Luke's Gospel until the procession of Palm Sunday, when the crowd blesses Jesus as king! (Luke 19:38). The presence of shepherds peering down over the slats of the manger brings strong memories—and great hopes—of one who will feed the flock, as Ezekiel once hoped, with justice. That is, after all, the meaning of the Hebrew word for shepherd: one who feeds, one who nourishes. The shepherds of Bethlehem understood that element of their vocation. Did they also glimpse this night's hopes that the mangered child would feed the flock given to his shepherding?

The second of Advent's choruses, the shepherds, moves across the stage. They talk, they share, they leave, they sing. They do not linger long enough to ask how this experience will change them, perhaps because we hear all we need to know. They have heard and responded, even though flocks required care and the rush across the fields might have been a bit dangerous in the dark. May we, like the shepherds, not be too sheepish to miss out on opportunities to see and to serve the Christ who has come.

FOR FURTHER REFLECTION

- When, and why, have you ever been so overwhelmed with joy or curiosity that you set aside all regular responsibilities to go and see and celebrate?
- What hopes for God's shepherding of persons and society does Advent awaken in you?

CAROL FOR THE DAY—"Rise Up, Shepherd, and Follow"

Day 3

— THE MAGI —

Revealers
MATTHEW 2:1-12

Westward leading, still proceeding,
guide us to thy perfect light.

In the early 1960s, when the effects of Biblical criticism
were beginning to be felt on a practical level, disbelief
in the magi was used by reactionaries as a barometer to
test just "how far out" an exegete was....It is told that
one such magi-debunker received a hand-painted
Christmas card depicting three very angry Orientals in
royal garb, accompanied by camels, knocking at the
door of his study, demanding by name to see him.
Raymond E. Brown, *The Birth of the Messiah*, 197–98

The Magi or wise men have become revered characters in the Christmas drama, as the anecdote above attests. Perhaps such reverence owes to the way these figures lend an exotic air to our pageants, where children wrap themselves in swaths of gaudy embossed draperies and carry to the baby Jesus glass bottles that once contained aftershave or perfume. Or perhaps the reverence stems from the way in which the Magi add to the Christmas stage a sense of mystery and allure, yet another unexpected embodiment of the Gospel's good news for all.

So who were the Magi? *Magi* is the Greek word used to identify Babylonian astrologers in Jesus' time. In English, the word survives in *magician,* magic being yet another of the activities attributed to this cast of sages. Only in Matthew's infancy story do Gentile stargazers play a prominent role. Over the centuries, perhaps to take away some of the scandal of having astrologers so close to the gospel's inauguration, the church began referring to these individuals as wise men or kings. Other traditions developed: from the number of gifts came the numbering of Magi or kings at three, in spite of the fact that earlier traditions spoke of numbers ranging from two to twelve. The names Balthasar, Caspar, and Melchior gradually won out over other options. Also added was the racial interpretation that Balthasar was Arabian, Caspar Indian, and Melchior Persian.

Whatever their precise number or identity, most important to this story and to Matthew's Gospel as a whole is the revelation that the Magi are Gentiles. In Matthew, addressed originally to a Jewish-Christian audience, the first to come and worship Jesus are Gentiles. This revealing of God's Christ to those outside the covenant even gives the season following Christmas its name, *epiphany,* from the Greek word that means to reveal or manifest. The Magi take center stage in Matthew because, while Jesus is born a Jew and focuses his primary ministry among the people of Israel, God's coming in Christ is of universal significance. *All* peoples will be the beneficiaries of this newborn king—a point of theology that likely spurred the legendary detail about the three kings each representing a different race.

The Magi's actions within the story also prove revealing in and of themselves. They may be stargazers, but they are not mind readers. They possess no special knowledge that allows them to go directly to Bethlehem, directly to the child. Instead the Magi have to rely on conventional wisdom: If we would find a king, we must go to a palace. Some naivete may even be attributed to the Magi: dealing with stars and charts all their lives, they may not have understood, much less ever dealt with, the likes of Herod before. If any truth of kingship resides in the old legends, it would be difficult to believe they had not heard of Herod. Herod had ruled now for nearly forty years with the favor and sanction of Rome. And Herod had not refrained from putting wife and son to the sword when he needed to hold onto power. One would not go and inquire of such a person about a new king born to the Jews, especially when the old king still has sting and venom.

The tradition that these were men of books and charts, with their eyes on the world above them and not necessarily around them, seems true enough when they counsel with Herod over the time of the star's appearance. The wisdom of the wise does not always perceive that the sharing of such information might be used in the plotting not of stars but death. So they give Herod the knowledge he seeks and continue on to the town identified by the scribes: Bethlehem.

As the Magi kneel before Jesus, their story takes the familiar turn to gold, frankincense, and myrrh. Gold as a gift for a king we understand. Perhaps even frankincense presents no difficulty, whose sweet-smelling aroma when burned could be used in the service of enthronement, where incense of all manner might rise and mingle and provide a sense of the unearthly. But myrrh? Myrrh appears to be an extraordinarily strange gift for an infant. It would be akin to coming to a niece's or nephew's first birthday party with a brightly wrapped box containing a cemetery plot deed or a prepaid Purple Cross plan in her or his name. We don't do that with children! At the beginning of their life we don't give them a gift that anticipates their dying!

Yet with myrrh that is what the Magi do. They reveal in the narrative and on the Christmas stage that this play consists of several acts and that even now a cross looms—not as an accident, not as a last-minute devising of how things can be addressed. No, myrrh reveals to characters and audience alike that death is central to the drama involving this child.

But not yet. As the story closes, the chorus comprised by the Magi heads out stage left after Herod has distinctly told them to leave stage right and return to him. Why? Did the wise men figure out the plot, the trap, the snare? No, one or more of them had a dream. Like many other biblical figures stretching all the way back to Jacob and soon to include Joseph, God intervenes for someone's sake through the experience of a dream. And deliverance comes.

For a moment let's listen to some of the elements of this story as if they were completely new to us: Gentile stargazers, vengeful kings, a gift suggesting death given to an infant, dream interpretation. We do not stand here on familiar ground. Little if any of this provides a scenario we might expect for the God of Israel to act and seek redemption. Yet that is the story woven by Matthew in these intriguing ways.

What does the chorus of Gentile stargazers we respectfully call Magi bring to the stage then? Their presence reveals, first of all, that God's coming in Christ stretches the boundaries even further than outcast—but still *Jewish*—shepherds. Gentiles come and worship at the outset. Seeds are sown for a church worldwide and all-inclusive. Second, the Magi reveal that wisdom is not always all it is cracked up to be. Their wisdom does not allow them to bypass Jerusalem and head straight for Bethlehem. Their wisdom does not even enable them to see through Herod's devices and his use of them. Only a dream given of God saves the day. Last, the Magi reveal at the Gospel's beginning the death to be endured as part of its completion.

The chorus of the Magi leaves the stage as mysteriously as it entered, following a dream much as the wise ones had followed a star. The star led to worshipful fulfillment. What the dream led to we do not know precisely. We know only that it did not lead to Herod. Indirectly it led to the child's living to grow into the man. Indirectly, one might also argue, it resulted not in one child's death but the death of many. Even the wisdom of sages cannot decipher or deter a king bent on evil. As the Magi chorus leaves, the chorus of the Innocents enters, taking its silent place on the stage, a place where even myrrh cannot mask the grotesque nature of Herod's revenge.

FOR FURTHER REFLECTION

- Who today reveals to you that God's coming in Christ is for all peoples?
- In what ways will you and your faith community's Advent observances point not only to the birth but to the sacrifice of Christ?

CAROL FOR THE DAY—"We Three Kings"

Day 4

—THE INNOCENTS—

Martyrs
MATTHEW 2:12-18

Then woe is me, poor child, for thee....

*C*hristmas and dreams. Think about how those two flow together so naturally, especially for children. *The Nutcracker Suite* draws its music and ballet from a child's dreaming of toys come to life. A clergyman's poem, originally known as "A Visit from St. Nicholas," begins with this scene:

> *The children were nestled all snug in their beds,*
> *While visions of sugar plums danced in their heads.*

Consider the first night of Christmas and the dreams of Mary and Joseph for their new baby. Shepherds initially interrupted those dreams when they shouldered and excused their way into the stable, excitedly stammering something about angels and manger, child and savior. Dreams would later toss those words and thoughts together with previous words and promises about the Child, as dreams often mesh and mix our experiences.

We might consider the dreams of other parents that night in Bethlehem for their children, for infant or expected daughters and sons with a lifetime ahead of them. Those dreams may have been of one child's continuing the family business or of another child's better fortunes in a new vocation. Perhaps some dreamt of their child becoming a teacher of God's Torah. In the days and months that followed Christmas, those dreams would continue and grow—and face reality.

Our text from Matthew reveals that other more ominous dreams unsettled the land. King Herod, who had ruled with more than a proverbial iron fist for over thirty years, had been disturbed by the visit of Magi from the East who had come looking for a new king born to the Jews. Such news did not sit well with Herod, who harbored his own dreams of continuing in power for long years to come. And at this point the Christmas dreams suddenly take on more the nature of a threatening nightmare as Matthew opens our text:

> *And having been warned in a dream not to return to Herod,*
> *[the Magi] left for their own country by another road. Now*
> *after they had left, an angel of the Lord appeared to Joseph in*
> *a dream and said, "Get up, take the child and his mother, and*
> *flee to Egypt, and remain there until I tell you; for Herod is*
> *about to search for the child, to destroy him."*

No longer are Christmas dreams the stuff of sugar plums and magical toys or even the aspirations of life's potential. The dreams have turned to matters of life and death, and the dreams are taken seriously. The wise men and the holy family flee, one to the east and one to the south, to escape the nightmare of Herod's jealousy. Both find sanctuary, but what of Bethlehem's other families? While Joseph tosses and turns with the troubling warning, what dreams do the other parents receive? What dances in the heads of their children that night when Herod coolly dispatches assassins of young children?

Whatever the dreams of parent or child, they are soon to be cruelly overwhelmed in the least understood and most ignored portion of the Christmas story in the Gospels:

> *When Herod saw that he had been tricked by the wise men,*
> *he was infuriated, and he sent and killed all the children in*

and around Bethlehem who were two years old or under,
according to the time that he had learned from the wise men.

The sound heard in Bethlehem was the shattering of dreams, a sound made even more deafening by its ensuing silence: the silence of young voices never more to be raised, the silence of loving words that could never more be heard, the silence of children sacrificed to the whims of madness. It is an awful story, not only because of the proximity of the stories of Jesus' birth to the innocents' death or because the church memorialized the Feast of Holy Innocents on the third day after Christmas. The truly awe-filled element of the narrative comes in discerning that Bethlehem's other children die in Jesus' place.

So what are we to make of these children, these innocents, as we set the stage that will unfold on Christmas? Sometimes the church omits this text's reading from the season because it doesn't fit in with the festive mood in which we are all supposed to be enraptured at this time of year. Some scholars have raised questions about its authenticity, pointing to the fact that the massacre is unattested to in any other extrabiblical source. But the story of the Innocents, the chorus they bring to the stage, cries out to be heard.

The story of Bethlehem's other children has much to teach us about the violence done to children and other innocents in our own time by those obsessed with positions and power politics. Herod's despicable action was not unique. In Africa children routinely serve as foot soldiers in campaigns waged in regions generally ignored by the media. Other regions, including the Middle East, have used children in combat roles. The violence in our own nation, by and against children, goes on every day. Children continue to be the ones most vulnerable, most easily victimized, and too often sacrificed. Scholars can argue the historicity of Herod's act, but it is a truth-telling story about what happens too often to this world's innocents.

The chorus of the Innocents does not just speak a parable for our time. In its movement comes a revelation to the world in general and the gospel in particular. We cannot read this story and conclude that life is fair. No last-minute rescue occurs. No footnote adds that Bethlehem really didn't have that many boys aged two years and under, as if that would make the act any less obscene. No explanation rationalizes that the children or the parents deserved special punishment. The tragedy simply occurs. The gospel, even Christmas, is not about things always turning out right in our time or in our sight.

The gospel *is* about God's gracious gift of life to us in the beloved child born in a manger. That same child will one day find his place and ministry, totally innocent, among two thieves. The irony of Matthew's Christmas story is that Jesus lives, while innocent children die in his place to satisfy the whim of a tyrant. Perhaps as Jesus expends himself in ministry and ultimately on the cross, he recalls the stories told to him by Joseph and Mary of these martyrs.

Such remembrances could have deepened Jesus' empathy for those he knew to be God's children. Indeed, Bethlehem's other children might have helped develop Jesus' closeness to and respect for children. To such as these, he later taught, belong God's sovereign realm.

So may we remember the innocents of Bethlehem. May we do so in efforts to protect the children of our time. May we do so to keep a place open on this stage for the chorus that reminds us of looming shadows that eventually link Christmas with Easter. And may we remember the innocents whose suffering anticipated that of the child with whom they once toddled and played on Bethlehem's streets—and with whom they now dwell in light, joy, and safety.

For Further Reflection

- What does this story of innocents' dying in the place of Jesus evoke in you?
- How will you remember the innocents this Advent and Christmas?

Carol for the Day—"Coventry Carol"

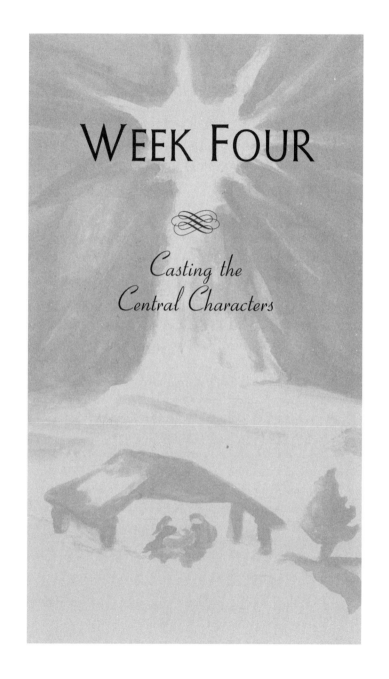

WEEK FOUR

*Casting the
Central Characters*

Practically every theatrical production relies upon several key characters who stand at the core of the drama and its plot. These are the ones about whom we care most by story's end, for these are the ones who have conveyed most to us, in positive or negative ways, the drama's tale.

In Advent, four such characters come to take their rightful places at center stage. Mary precedes all by virtue of her trusting acceptance that sets the plot of birth in motion. Joseph follows, a man renowned for his righteousness yet given to trusting dreams that enable the receiving and saving of life. Not surprisingly, the Child numbers among these main characters, the Child whose birth serves as fulfillment to many promises and is the genesis for many others. And God takes the stage, not as the last character introduced, for actually God is the one who has been moving this drama all along. Placing God at center stage at the end simply reminds us of that gracious fact, of providence winding its way from prophets and before to mangers and beyond.

Watch and listen as these characters take their places. Avoid allowing the familiarity we have with them to stifle a fresh hearing of their stories in this drama. Christmas itself relies upon the elements of wonder and surprise. Keep those qualities in mind and heart as these four readings conclude the setting of the Christmas stage.

$\mathcal{D}ay$ 1

MARY

One Who Trusts
LUKE 1:26-38

God lifted up my lowliness in many marvelous ways.

*G*od whispered, and a silence fell; the world poised one expectant moment." So begins a poem entitled "The Annunciation" by Theodosia Garrison. We may associate the speaking of God with thundering displays, not unlike the scene in *The Wizard of Oz* when the booming sound effects of the wizard hidden behind the curtains frightens Dorothy and her companions out of their wits. Occasional biblical narratives do record the speaking of God's word as a shaking of the very ground upon which the saints of old stood.

Yet the picture—and sound—of the Annunciation differs from that. The word of God through the messenger Gabriel comes without fanfare, comes without rush of wind or quaking of earth. Rather, in the image of the poem, we see and hear the whispered voice of God, words softly spoken so as not to frighten the young girl. "Greetings, favored one! The Lord is with you." And then, silence. The compact way in which the biblical narrative proceeds may do violence to the actual progression of time and emotions in this text. Luke records at this point that Mary "was much perplexed by [the angel's] words and pondered what sort of greeting this might be." In a classic painting of the Annunciation, Mary reclines on a couch. An unannounced and unexpected visitor who stands next to her startles Mary from rest. The artist enables us to see her almost drawing back from this presence. The pause is caught in her eyes. She looks not at the visitor nor even at the viewer of the painting. Rather her stare goes out beyond all, a wide-eyed look of wonderment and bewilderment that moves the viewer to turn to see what she might be seeing or hearing.

We may safely assume that Gabriel genuinely startles the young woman Mary, who is unprepared for the visitor, a visitor who, by the way, does not introduce himself by name or identity. Luke only says who (and what) he is for the benefit of the reader. Mary takes in the message then, not on the basis of familiarity (*I know your name*) or even authority (*I know you're an angel*). Mary hears his word and makes her decision of acceptance on the sole basis of trusting in the God of Israel, for that authority is the only one to which the visitor appeals. Mary's trust—and *trust* is simply another word for faith—sets the stage for her participation in the truly radical announcement about the child's identity and authority:

> *You will conceive in your womb and bear a son, and you will name him Jesus. He will be great, and will be called the Son of the Most High…the child to be born will be holy; he will be called Son of God.*

The news given Mary rings familiar to our ears. But be assured that it came as news to Mary, who did not have the luxury that comes from the hindsight of our annual retelling of the Christmas story. Despite apocryphal legends concerning her childhood and even later theologies of her own immaculate conception, Mary most likely had as much experience with angelic visitors as anyone now reading this book. For her, a true daughter of Israel, such events belonged to times past when God spoke to patriarchs and matriarchs and sent them angel messengers. But there seemed to have been a long period of angelic and prophetic silence since those times.

Even more troubling, these words given to Mary, which we hear so casually year in and year out, would have sounded a clear note of offense within Judaism. In its strict monotheism, God is Wholly Other. To speak of a *Son of God* in Judaism draws dangerously close to blasphemy. Symbolically, Jews could accept the term. Literally, the idea of God's siring a human child would offend religious sensibilities. In Mary's time divine/human beings would have represented a heresy associated with the pagan religions. Judaism rejected such mingling. Let others serve their gods and goddesses or their divinities with human consorts. We will serve the One God.

Mary, a daughter of Israel, could have rejected outright, with the best of theological reasons, any such notion of a Son of the Most High—much less bearing such a child herself. Yet Mary's response to such an incredible word is not one of incensed repudiation but a simple question: "How can this be, since I am a virgin?" The simplicity of Mary's faith breaks through. Her question turns not on theological disagreement but biological uncertainty, pointing to a remarkable openness on Mary's part to the way of God in life. Several times in his book the prophet Isaiah urged Israel on behalf of God, "Do not remember the former things, or consider the things of old. I am about to do a new thing" (Isa. 43:18-19). Mary's faith demonstrates Isaiah's openness to the new ways of God, in history in general and within her own life in particular. It is one thing to affirm that God is free to do as God wills in this world. The real crunch comes in allowing God the freedom and trust to act in one's own life. Mary gives God that room.

Mary's question of "how" receives response, though not precise answer, in the angel's closing words: "For nothing will be impossible with God." What the angel leaves unsaid in those words of assurance and hope is perhaps more eloquent than what is spoken. What will be impossible for a God who has brought this entire universe into being, a God who now looks with grace upon a young woman from a frontier town in a fourth-rate country at the margins of a harsh empire? Mary hears the word borne by the angel, and her response opens her to bear the Word God would speak in the flesh: "Here am I, the servant of the Lord; let it be with me according to your word." Without fully realizing or understanding where such an act of faith will lead her, Mary opens her life to the plans of God. Those plans will eventually involve the whole world, but for now they begin with "Let it be."

"God whispered, and a silence fell." God's coming does not require drumrolls and cymbal crashes or a messenger with wings sprouting from shoulders; but in the stillness, through the unexpected, God may come to us.

Mary sets the Christmas stage by revealing the way its gift comes through and to those who trust. May we, like Mary, offer the simple trust of humble servants, willing to let God's ever-fresh possibilities come to be in our lives. God still whispers words of grace and vocation, a whispering soon to be heard again in the soft cooing of a Child in a manger. God give us ears to hear and lives to offer to that Incarnate Word.

FOR FURTHER REFLECTION

- How have you experienced God's addressing you with words of favor or vocation?

- What might your faith need to "let it be" this Advent?

CAROL FOR THE DAY—"My Soul Gives Glory to My God"

$\mathcal{D}ay$ 2

—————— JOSEPH ——————

Follower of Dreams
MATTHEW 1:18-25; 2:13-15

Gentle Joseph, Joseph dear, stay with me, for the baby's near.

D reamers. In Western society few seek the label of "dreamer" as a description of character or work ethic. "Just a dreamer" dismisses those who may think good thoughts or develop innovative plans but who never quite translate them into deed or action.

Yet if no one ever dreams of what could be, how will new ways come? "Think tanks," whether political or business, allow individuals the time, space, and support not only to study and investigate—but to dream. Many advances in the computer industry came from those who did not first tinker with the hardware but who speculated (dreamed) how to translate ideas into programs that would take shape in the software that would run the hardware that would accomplish the tasks or enable the games. All this stems from the following of dreams.

Conventional wisdom holds that the chief importance of Joseph to the Christmas stage derives from his Davidic background that links him to Bethlehem. Yet another key interpretive piece of information for understanding the place of Joseph on this stage is his name, Joseph. We have encountered that name before in the biblical text. In the formative stories of Genesis, Joseph was the favored son of Jacob, the possessor of the many-colored coat. A series of adventures (and misadventures!) surrounds Joseph. But the one defining element of Joseph was this: He was a dreamer and one given to the interpretation of dreams. Joseph dreamed and got in trouble with his brothers because of them. Joseph interpreted the dreams of cell mates and eventually found his way out of prison because of it. Joseph interpreted the dreams of Pharaoh, and he became second in the land. Why? Because Joseph's interpreting of dreams led to action, and the action saved life.

Dreams led to action, and the action saved life.

Joseph's namesake in Matthew 1 faces a difficult issue. His betrothed, Mary, is found to be pregnant. Matthew lightens the scandal by indicating the pregnancy resulted "from the Holy Spirit." That footnote surely comes from the safety of hindsight. In the eyes of Joseph, uncertainty surrounds Mary's being with child, not the least of which is, What to do now?

The description of Joseph as "righteous" does not make that choice any easier; in fact, it complicates his decision. Those judged to be the righteous or just in Judaism lived by the law. And in this case, the law was clear. Betrothal represented a binding arrangement, whose breach was considered adulterous. Deuteronomy 22:23-27 designated the punishment in such cases: death. By the time of Matthew's writing, other rabbinic teachings said execution was not the only option—but it did remain the chief one. So when Matthew writes that Joseph is "unwilling to expose her to public disgrace, [and] planned to dismiss her quietly," we learn that Joseph possesses a compassionate nature. But only in the following verses do we discover that Joseph, like his namesake before him, is also a dreamer— and a man willing to act upon dreams. His dream this night takes the form of an angel who says to set fear aside and take Mary as wife. According to the dream, the child is a work of God's own Spirit, a child who will come to save people.

Consider for a moment the position in which this message places Joseph. To follow this dream, at best, risks the ridicule of his community for being weak in dealing with Mary's perceived infidelity. At worst it threatens to bring the community's censure upon him, for without Joseph's condemnation of Mary, gossips logically would assume that he also has broken the covenant of betrothal by fathering the child. Yet Joseph chooses to follow dreams rather than conventions.

So Joseph stands with Mary, stands with the dream, and receives the child as his own. Dreams are difficult to follow in this life, easily dashed by disappointments or those who do not live up to expectations, easily misunderstood by those who are not privy to their meaning. But Joseph dreams and follows the dream. And as with Joseph of old, life is saved. Mary lives, who might otherwise have died at the hands of those bent on following the letter of the law. And the child within her lives, who was as vulnerable then as when he nestled in the manger.

But let us not forget Joseph's second dream. Following the visit of the Magi, Joseph dreams again. Only now the word warns that home and even country be left for an indefinite time. Joseph the dreamer must choose whether to become Joseph the pilgrim, the exile, and whether to inflict that hardship upon wife and son. The identification of Herod with the threat surely lent other complications. Herod's long arm could certainly reach to Egypt through his alliances. Why flee to a place where no one could be trusted? Why not at least stay where the dangers would be relatively known? The dream offers no words to such concerns. Its acceptance and following requires trust in the One who offers it.

Once more Joseph wakes and acts upon the dream. Once more he saves life by taking mother and child in a hasty flight to the same land where his namesake had once been led in chains. Joseph of old never left that land, not until centuries later when his descendants fulfilled a promise exacted from his brothers to bear his bones back to the land of promise (Gen. 50:24) when Israel finally made that journey home.

Matthew's Joseph received no time line in the dream as to the length of this exile. A year or two or ten: that too involved trusting and following. The consequences of dreams do not always work with clockwork precision. Dreams of justice and mercy may take years or lifetimes or more to unfold. Our dream of God's sovereign realm, offered in the prayer of Jesus each time we raise it, stretches far beyond our lifetimes. Yet, like Joseph's dream, our dream seeks not merely our idle reflection but our action and embodiment.

On the Christmas stage, Joseph serves to remind us that the dreams of Christmas await persons willing to follow dreams. We often sing of those dreams in this season: of peace on earth and God's favor toward creation, of a little child who leads us and a Sovereign who comes to save rather than dominate. Joseph gives us this glimpse of the Christmas dream accepted and followed. May we have the courage to dream the dreams of God: dreams that save life, dreams that give hope, dreams that lift us up and move us on to where God would have us go!

FOR FURTHER REFLECTION

- What dreams does this season engender in you?
- How will you speak and act in Advent and beyond to help bring those dreams to fruition?

CAROL OF THE DAY—"Gentle Joseph, Joseph Dear"

Day 3

——— THE CHILD ———

One Who Fulfills

MATTHEW 1:22-23, 25; LUKE 2:7

Why lies he in such mean estate where ox and ass are feeding?

*I*n classic theatrical staging, much depends on the action and plot all moving to a critical and decisive climax. Questions are finally answered. Relationships are at last revealed in their true light. In tragedy this climax serves as the point where catastrophe occurs. In comedy goodness and laughter achieve a conclusive triumph over whatever has been prevailed against. The climax tends to reveal the playwright's purpose for crafting the drama in the first place.

Thus far in setting the Christmas stage we have explored backdrops that define the breadth of this drama, scenery that provides a sense of color and time and choruses that bring key voices to the plot. In this chapter we have cast two of the central characters on the stage, Joseph and Mary, who have taught us lessons of trust, dreaming, and acceptance. In terms of the Christmas drama, however, the climax has not yet been reached. Another character needs to appear, though in a most unlikely fashion. This one will bring no moving soliloquy or engage in any spirited onstage action that turns the tide against the foes. This one enters the stage cooing and gurgling, with all the attendant helplessness and vulnerability of any other newborn child. Jesus, the child.

Now some might object to seeing the birth as climax to this

drama. Is it not the beginning? In the life of Jesus of Nazareth, yes. But in the setting of the Christmas stage, the birth of Jesus seals the story and makes it whole.

Both of the Gospels that narrate Jesus' birth do so in the most terse of manners, almost *anti*climactically. One finds none of the legends here as in the apocryphal gospels, of light brighter than the sun or the healing of a midwife when she touches the infant. Instead, Luke and Matthew matter of factly record the birth with precious few details. But one aspect of those details reveals why the birth of this child is rightly the climax of the story unfolding on the Christmas stage: fulfillment. We know fulfillment looms large because of Matthew 1:22, "All this took place to *fulfill* what had been spoken." And while Luke does not use the word *fulfill* in his account, we shall shortly see why fulfillment looms large there.

First, how does Luke's verse about Jesus' birth connect with fulfillment? When the angel later speaks to the shepherds, he gives them a sign by which they will recognize that the joy and good news spoken can be trusted and that their fears can be set aside. That sign consists of a child wrapped in bands of cloth and lying in a manger. The shepherds rush to Bethlehem, and the words find fulfillment in what they see there.

But let us not rush off this point, especially since we are so familiar with bands of cloth ("swaddling cloths") and a manger through years of Christmas services, pageants, and readings. The fulfillment of God's promises in a child lying in a manger would not have been the obvious choice to position the pinnacle of the Christmas drama. It certainly would not have been so for first-century shepherds who had no cause to think of the birth of royalty in squalor and no tradition of hearing this story recited year in and year out to take away its scandal. The mangered child represents an overturning of old ways.

And the bands of cloth? In first-century Palestine peasant women wrapped infants in cloth, believing it would help keep the child's limbs straight. When the shepherds saw the child so wrapped, they not only saw a fulfillment of the angel's words; they saw by all appearances an ordinary child. *Good news, great joy, Savior, Messiah*: All those wonderful words spoken from the night sky, here they found wrapped in cloths like one of their own. Sometimes we need Jesus not to be so different from us. Sometimes we need to see Christ taking our form, experiencing our lives so that we may be understood, loved, and accepted by One who knows us and our lives from the inside. Jesus, wrapped and swaddled, fulfills that need.

Matthew traces the birth of Jesus as fulfillment to the seventh chapter of Isaiah. Over the centuries, the church has often focused its attention exclusively on but one of the Hebrew words used in that text: *almah*. Does it mean "virgin" in this context, or does it simply mean "young woman"? Persons of faith have interpreted it both ways, as the Hebrew allows. But a far more pressing issue of fulfillment in this text quoted by Matthew comes not in Mary's biological condition but in her child's identity: "'They shall name him Emmanuel,' which means 'God is with us.'" Matthew sees the birth of Jesus fulfilling the prophecy of Emmanuel, God with us.

The fulfillment of Emmanuel in Jesus reveals why the Christmas stage reaches its climax in the birth story. All of the ways God has come and sought to be present to God's people, through law and prophets, through liturgy and sacred places: All now come to fruition, to fulfillment, in the birth cry of Jesus. In this child God's place on the stage becomes something it has never been before in history. The next reading will spend more time on God's presence on the Christmas stage and in human history. But for now suffice it to say that the child has come—and through that child, God is with us as never before.

For Mary and Joseph the birth of Jesus brought fulfillment of hopes for a child not unlike the fulfillment other parents experience at the birth of a child, especially a firstborn. But given Mary's experience in the Annunciation and Joseph's dream, other fulfillments accompanied that birth in their lives. Likewise, in the birth of Jesus we may begin to look for and see glimpses of other fulfillments. Perhaps they have not been reached as yet. Perhaps they belong to other narratives still being written, even awaiting our own participation. But in Jesus' birth, God's sovereign realm announces that its territory stretches to where you and I live.

That breadth of God's love is what the shepherds discovered, seeing the infant resting in conditions no different from the poverty they and their families knew, looking for all the world like one of their own children. That is what Matthew perceived, discerning that the child whose birth initially raised serious questions to Joseph about fidelity was actually the One whose birth fulfilled God's promise (an act of fidelity!) of Emmanuel, of a God-entered and God-beloved world. In the child of Bethlehem, we find the one who is not only Christ and Savior of the whole world but the one who has come among us and dwells in our midst even now.

What child is this? This, this, is Christ the Lord! May God be praised for the great gift of Jesus' birth, the child who brings life to all.

FOR FURTHER REFLECTION

- What fulfillment does Jesus' birth accomplish or anticipate in your life?
- What details of Jesus' birth intrigue you or shape your faith the most?

CAROL FOR THE DAY—"What Child Is This"

Day 4

GOD

One Who Comes
ISAIAH 42:14-16; JOHN 1:1-5, 14

*Joy to the world, the Lord is come!...
let every heart prepare [God] room.*

Theater relies almost inevitably upon words, upon speech. Backdrops and scenery may provide insights into mood and setting. Action may embody choices. But in terms of interpretation and the expression of fine details, words provide drama with spirit and depth, whether in stage instructions or dialogue or soliloquy. The Christmas stage is no different. And as we encounter the God who comes to us upon this stage, we learn again of the importance of words...and Word.

In these readings past, we have looked at the Christmas stage from a variety of angles and characters. But what was Christmas for God? What meaning and consequence did Christmas have on God's existence, purpose, and joy? The two texts above provide a way to discern the place of God upon the Christmas stage.

In Isaiah 42 the prophet addressed the community of Israel in exile, a community that faced new choices with the disintegration of the Babylonian empire and the possibilities for return to the promised land. For some grown comfortable and even somewhat prosperous in exile, such an overturning of the status quo seemed threatening. But to others, like the author of this chapter, the changes represented the intervention of God in history. Listen to the opening imagery of the text, and hold it in balance within the context of the Christmas stage. The voice of the text represents not that of the prophet but of God.

> For a long time I have held my peace,
>   I have kept still and restrained myself;
> now I will cry out like a woman in labor,
>   I will gasp and pant.

Isaiah understood the end of exile and the beginnings of return that will issue from the ending of God's silence in a cry depicted as nothing less than the birth-shout of a mother. Again, hold those words alongside the God encountered upon the Christmas stage. There too silence finds its breaking in a birth cry. And there too God brings life, not just to a mother, but to a people and even a whole creation through the birthing that takes place at Christmas.

This image of God's breaking silence speaks profoundly to an Israel who had grown accustomed to a prophetic silence. Long before Isaiah, Amos had pronounced a judgment involving not a famine of bread but of "hearing the words of the Lord." Many believed that the prophetic voice had been stilled since the time of Ezra and Nehemiah. God seemed to have stood silent—but no longer. The Christmas stage echoes with the voice of God who cries out in joy and hope at Jesus' birth.

This breaking of God's silence possesses the possibility of renewing hope in folks who find themselves dwelling in places of silence: silence brought by illness or estrangement, while living under oppression or amidst sheer loneliness. The church finds part of her calling in serving as a sounding board for God's silence-breaking, hope-giving voice. Such service, of course, requires that we move among those who experience the silence, the alienation, the hopelessness. We cannot wait for those so afflicted to find their way to us. God sought out creation on the Christmas stage, giving us the example and challenge to go and do likewise.

The other text noted above comes at the opening of John's Gospel, which, like Mark's, contains none of the traditional stories associated with Christmas. No angels descend from the sky to offer signs and songs. No shepherds leave flocks behind to rush across the Bethlehem fields to see for themselves what has been told them. No Magi journey across the landscape, following the movement of stars to discern and then search out a new king. Neither Mary nor Joseph appears. John's Gospel concerns itself with the appearance of the word of God—a Word whose place and speaking on the Christmas stage provides some unique insights into the God who comes to us.

"In the beginning...." With those words, John intentionally places the opening of his Gospel alongside the opening words of the biblical witness. In those first words of beginnings in Genesis, the story spoke of creation's unfolding from God's hand and purpose. In the Gospel of John, these new words of beginnings portend a new creation emerging from those same hands and purposes. The Word present at creation's beginning, the Word now become flesh to live among us, John identifies not only *with* God; this Word *was* God, according to the prologue. In Jesus of Nazareth, as a relatively recent affirmation of faith puts it, God has come and shared our common lot.

Until this moment on the Christmas stage, God had largely been known "from above." God had, as John intimates, created the universe and human life. God had spoken to Israel through law and prophets, from burning bushes and leading clouds. Even God's immanence, once experienced in the Ark of the Covenant, had a strong dose of separation characterized in the death of those who touched it in accidental ways.

Once exile came, the Ark disappeared. But now John perceives an extraordinary turn of events. While God had remained wrapped in the awe and mystery known fully only by the Word, that Word has now become flesh. That Word has come to make God known and to bring life to all people by revealing God. In Jesus Christ the Word of God, Emmanuel lives incarnate.

The God who comes on the Christmas stage works such a miracle. Perhaps that explains why we wrap this season with so many trappings: lights and crèches, trees and carols, decorations and customs, candles and ornaments. None can contain the truth, for none can contain the miracle of God with us.

That miracle remains for us to experience by opening our lives to the God who still would come to us. Even on our off days, even when we cannot see stars or do not feel like singing carols, even then, God's love incarnate seeks in us a dwelling, a birthing, where our spirits may be filled with the Word whose light shines in any and all darkness.

Look around at the stage that has been set for Christmas. Prophets surround us. Living scenes beckon us. Choruses enlighten us. Mary, Joseph, and Child teach us. And God? God has come to show us love unbounded in its mercy, unfettered by its reach, and unyielding for its purpose of our recreation in the child born for us and for all. For, as the carol puts it, God comes to make God's blessings flow!

So let the people say, *Amen* . . . and *Merry Christmas*!

FOR FURTHER REFLECTION

- How have you experienced the promise of Emmanuel, "God with us," in your life?
- How might this reading shape your Christmas celebration?

CAROL OF THE DAY—"Joy to the World"

E PILOGUE

A Reading for Christmas Day

The Word became flesh, and lived among us...

The crowds that beset Bethlehem bustled early that morning. All sought to gain a favorable position in the line winding around to the census-taker's booth. Their premature rising had been spurred by a cold night, where every star imaginable glistened with heatless light. The chill of dawn's crisp air quickened more than a few streetbound sojourners to exchange bedroll cocoons for the piling of sticks and striking of flints. For pilgrims scattered throughout the village, hope gained momentum that this would be the day when business with Caesar's officials could be transacted and journeys home then begun.

But in one corner of the town, where the last lodging had been secured the evening before, grumblings of what sort of day this would be dominated the early meal's conversation. The night before had been anything but restful. Bad enough, some said, to have someone pounding on the door when quiet just settled in. Worse yet, replied others, when the ill-prepared Galilean outside wailed his sob story about a wife needing a place to rest. With sleeping mats totally covering the inn's floor already, nothing could be done. But the Galilean couldn't be reasoned with. Finally, more to silence him than help the woman, the innkeeper pointed out back, muttering something about bedding down with the other dumb beasts. He slammed the door shut. In a moment, a few brays and lows could be heard from the stable, signaling the couple's arrival. Then silence returned.

But not for long. In a short time, a woman's cries rang out from the stable—cries the innkeeper's wife soon recognized to be those of birthing. The tongue-lashing she administered to her husband woke any not roused by the stable sounds. "Is it you've no eyes to see when someone's full with child?" she sputtered, while gathering fresh clothes and clean water and a lamp, "Or no brains to understand?" Stepping over the bodies criss-crossed on the inn's floor, she made her way to the stable.

To those who managed to muster some concern and worry for the mother, the child's first cry came as welcome relief. To those merely annoyed by the commotion, it was just another nuisance in what had fast become a very *un*silent night.

Even then, there would have been time to gain suitable sleep before dawn, were it not for the other visitors that came in another hour or two. Shepherds, someone conjectured. And they very well might have been. No one heard them come, which would be in keeping with men accustomed to traveling stealthily to check on flocks and ward off danger. Shortly after their hushed coming, however, the noise began in earnest. Shouts and clapping, rough-spoken prayers and off-key songs sent the stable animals off into a barnyard cacophony.

Some speculated the noise stemmed from the shepherds' sipping too much from their wineskins to forget the cold. But the villagers' shouts for silence did nothing to dampen the herdsmen's gruff enthusiasm. Sounds of singing and laughter carried through the air long after they had gone. When they reached the crest of the hills to the east, it sounded as if their noise came down from the sky itself. That had to be the explanation. How else could the sound of rejoicing be heard as though it came from the stars that served as Bethlehem's mantle that night?

Needless to say, morning brought little sympathy for the new family. More than one passerby made pointed remarks about parents who cared so little for their child as to make such poor plans for his coming into the world. Such a child, with such a start, was surely destined for a miserable life, perhaps even a life that would drain their own resources. So much poverty in the land already put great demands on their charity. If only the poor would learn to take care of themselves—or at least their children.

In the stable, the morning's activities had begun as early as any in Bethlehem that day. Joseph had been busy at work from the moment of their taking shelter in the stable. First, in finding a suitable place for the birth and then the infant's bedding. Then in attending to the needs of wife and child. And of course, there were the animals.

Joseph had carpentered in stables before: patching roofs, adding new stalls, repairing yokes and other tools. In those times, he relied on the owner to clean up after the animals and see to their keeping. But now, with Mary and the newborn to think of, it fell to him to keep the stable a fit place for mother and child. Oddly, Joseph found it necessary to constantly shoo the animals from the manger, herding them to the corner where their food had been moved. But they kept coming back —the cow's slow loping, the sheep's brisker step, the dove's fluttered swoop—to peer over the manger at the child.

Joseph kept reminding himself it must be force of habit. Curiosity is a human emotion. Shepherds could be curious, not cattle or sheep. But the look on the shepherds' faces as they peered over the slats differed little from the faces of cattle, sheep, and dove that continued to wander in the child's direction. Such thoughts convinced Joseph he needed more sleep.

And the mother? Some of Joseph's admonitions to rest after the ordeal had their effect. Sleep would come and go. But the moment any noise from the child came forth—a slight rustling in the hay, a muffled whimper, a soft gurgling—Mary bolted as when that life first burst from her. But in the moments of quiet and rest, when even vigilant Joseph closed heavy eyes in sleep...in those moments, other thoughts occupied Mary's mind.

Those thoughts took her back months before, to a visit by one who brought strange words of blessing to her—and announced the mystery of a child called holy, even son of God. Thoughts that blended into her subsequent journey to cousin Elizabeth, who likewise spoke words difficult to comprehend but joyful to hear. Thoughts came of Joseph's recent decision not to put her away for the disgrace she'd brought to his name, a decision he confided came from a visit much like her own.

When Joseph woke her earlier with news of shepherds come to see a Child spoken of by sky-borne angels, Mary could not be certain she had not drifted off into an even deeper sleep. But their story convinced her not merely of her wakefulness; it also brought reassurance of her faithfulness. This miracle of life possessed an even more miraculous dimension. This miracle of life drawn from within her somehow embodied *the* miracle of life. That is what shepherds seemed to mean. That is what Elizabeth seemed to say. That is what the angel seemed to announce.

But how could this be? Life to the world in an infant lying in cattle fodder? Looking over at the wrinkled face nestled in the trough, Mary thought she would laugh. And she did. On Christmas morning, Mary laughed: not with disbelief but with recognition. Not with ridicule but joy. Mary laughed—and pondered how a Word once promised now squirmed with life in hay-cradled flesh.

APPENDIXES

Appendix One

FINDING THE CAROLS

This resource has suggested a carol for each day to use in preparation for or reflection on the reading. Where can you find the full text (or music) for the carols themselves, beyond the one-line quote used at the top of each reading?

The following compilation uses three sources that contain all but one of the carols mentioned in this book. The three sources are *The Presbyterian Hymnal* (PH), *The United Methodist Hymnal* (UMH), and *The New Century Hymnal* (NCH) of the United Church of Christ. Some of the more familiar carols appear in all three, others in one or two.

Other resources will prove equally valuable. Many families (and churches) have Christmas music recordings of many of these carols. If you have the equipment available for playback, listen to the carols to enhance the connection of these songs to the readings. Yet another resource is the Internet. For example, the one carol listed below that does not appear in any of the above hymnals is readily available on the Internet. I used a search engine for "Coventry Carol" to find not only text and music but the song being played.

Whether you use this resource and its carols in a private devotional setting, family gatherings, group studies, or wider congregational use, make use of the carols. Listen to them, not only for their words but for the tunes that have become attached to them. The music of this season helps set the Christmas stage, especially in ways that touch the emotions.

*(Carols listed in order of appearance in book; numbers
are pages in hymnals indicated above.)*

Prepare the Way	PH (13)
Come, Thou Long-Expected Jesus	UMH (196), PH (1, 2), NCH (122)
It Came upon the Midnight Clear	UMH (218), PH (38), NCH (131)
Watchman, Tell Us of the Night	PH (20), NCH (103)
People, Look East	UMH (202), PH (12)
In the Bleak Midwinter	UMH (221), PH (36), NCH (128)
The Friendly Beasts	UMH (227), NCH (138)
O Come, O Come, Emmanuel	UMH (211), PH (9), NCH (116)
Angels We Have Heard on High	UMH (238), PH (23), NCH (125)
Rise Up, Shepherd, and Follow	PH (50)
We Three Kings	UMH (254), PH (66)
Coventry Carol	(Not in any of these three hymnals)
My Soul Gives Glory to My God	UMH (198), PH (600), NCH (119)
Gentle Joseph, Joseph Dear	NCH (105)
What Child Is This	UMH (219), PH (53), NCH (148)
Joy to the World	UMH (246), PH (40), NCH (132)

Appendix Two

SUGGESTED
SESSION OUTLINES

Setting the Christmas Stage places the session guides in this appendix rather than in a separate leader's guide for two reasons. First, it intends to aid those who will be reading this book without benefit of a group experience. If you do so, consider reviewing the session guide for the chapter you have just read or are about to read. The same holds true for the third appendix on family and congregational activities. Let these suggested exercises provide added opportunities and angles from which to reflect on the stories and drama of Advent. Second, this design attempts to help those groups that will rotate leadership among several persons. If group members can access the same material ahead of time, hopefully folks will be more open to sharing in the leadership. This approach will also help your group find ways to involve more than one person in planning the sessions, if the group desires to do so.

The following outlines for group study sessions are guides for once-a-week studies during the four weeks of Advent. If Christmas falls within a day or two of the fourth Sunday in Advent, your group may wish to consider beginning the study the week before Advent begins. Decide well ahead of time so participants have ample time to work this study into their schedules. The sessions have been written with adults in mind. For a more intergenerational approach, incorporate some of the suggestions in Appendix Three for family observances as well as adapting the suggested session activities themselves.

Each session guide includes SESSION PREPARATION, LEADING THE SESSION, and WRAP-UP.

SESSION PREPARATION will identify resources and indicate arrangements to be made before the session. These preparations will include the development of worship centers, use of carols, and materials for craft or other hands-on activities.

LEADING THE SESSION will provide suggestions for activities and discussions during the session itself. This section will also introduce optional exercises, offering more than enough ideas to fill your time (the session assumes approximately one hour). Focus on those exercises that you believe will work best with your group; feel free to create your own activities to address the issues raised in each session. I only ask that when you make such changes you do not put words in the author's mouth (or pen). To achieve some continuity from session to session, each week's study will follow the same basic outline:

- Gathering by the Stage
- Exploring the Stage's Drama
- Finding Ourselves Onstage

WRAP-UP will focus on bringing closure to the session, passing along what has been done or addressed to the wider church as appropriate, and any assignments for the next week.

If your group has access to a study area adjacent to a stage, that would be ideal. However, any room or space can be made inviting and appropriate to *Setting the Christmas Stage* by following some of the suggestions below and by using your own creativity and imagination.

You may also wish to look at Appendix Three, suggestions for family and congregational observances or activities based on this book, for further ideas to include in your group.

Week One: Erecting the Backdrops

Session Preparation

PREPARE THE ROOM

Cut four long, narrow strips of paper (24" or longer), and print on them the names of the prophets in this chapter (one per strip). On the other side of the paper (or on four other strips), write the following words associated with each prophet in the study: *Preparation* (Isaiah), *Promise* (Jeremiah), *Peace* (Micah), *Messenger* (Malachi).

Display the banner strips where they will be in view during the session. If printed on both sides, hang from the ceiling with string so both sides can be read.

MATERIALS NEEDED

- Newsprint sheets, markers
- Hymnals or songbooks with the carol you will be using at the end of the session
- Tape or CD system and recordings to play carols in #1

OTHER PREPARATIONS

If you use the optional panel presentation in #4, work ahead of time with four adults (or three if you will be one of the panel members) to help plan the presentation.

Leading the Session

GATHERING BY THE STAGE

1. Welcome adults as they enter. Have carols from this week's readings playing in the background, if possible.

2. Direct adults to the newsprint sheets(s) and markers. Invite persons to write down preparations they will be making in the next several weeks to ready themselves, home, family, and church for Christmas. Encourage persons to be as thorough as possible.

3. Lead the group in a brief discussion of the list developed. Ask for silent reflection on which items cannot be separated from the awaited birth toward which this season moves. Offer this opening prayer or another of your own: *Holy God, help us make ready for your coming to us. May the words of preparation spoken by prophets of old take hold and take shape in lives made new by your Spirit's presence. In the name of the Christ who comes. Amen.*

EXPLORING THE STAGE'S DRAMA

4. Form four small groups. Assign to each group one of the prophets and the accompanying scripture readings for that prophet. Have groups read assigned texts, review materials in that text's reading, then report to others what they see as leading issues concerning Advent.

   Option: Have a panel presentation by persons taking the part of the four prophets, followed by an opportunity for the rest of the group to ask questions.

5. On another sheet of newsprint, write down key words and phrases that occur in these texts as reported out by the groups. Identify how these words and phrases have entered into contemporary Advent preparations.

FINDING OURSELVES ONSTAGE

6. Revisit the list created at the beginning of the session in light of the types of preparations announced by Isaiah and reflected on in this week's first reading. Discuss what items on the list persons might want to change or add or give greater emphasis.

7. Call attention to the readings on Jeremiah and Micah. Have the group consider ways this season portrays promises in general and peace in particular: for example, by the media, by political and social leaders, by the church. Identify similarities and differences among the depictions. Discuss how your church might play a role in your community that encourages promise keeping and peacemaking.

Option: Based on this last discussion, select a local project in which group members would like to participate as part of Advent's preparations. Make plans to carry it out (or at least initiate it) between now and Christmas.

8. Ask adults to reflect silently on persons who serve as Advent's "messengers" of change and hope for them. Ask adults to share thoughts with a partner.

    Option: Follow this sharing with a discussion by the whole group of who serves as Advent's messengers for those who live in crisis, for the unchurched, or for those without hope. Encourage adults to consider ways individuals and the church could serve in those roles, opening ourselves to such messengers.

Wrap-Up

9. Invite adults to offer one-word or single-phrase responses to this session.

10. Close by singing or reading "Watchman, Tell Us of the Night" or one of the other carols from this week's reading.

11. Remind adults to read the next week's texts and readings and to use the suggested carols as they are able.

    Talk to several group members afterward to get a better sense of how the session went. Incorporate their ideas into planning the next session.

Week Two: Constructing the Scenery

Session Preparation

PREPARE THE ROOM

Select symbols for each of the scenes considered in this week's readings: for example, sitting room (rocking chair, painting); inn (no vacancy sign, room rate card); stable (straw, live animal); throne room (crown, formal chair, sword). Place one symbol (or set of symbols) in each corner of the room. Plan ahead of time whether you will move the group to each corner with activities 5–8 or bring symbols into middle of the group.

MATERIALS NEEDED

- Butcher paper or newsprint to create a long (6') piece for a mural (tape or glue several sheets of newsprint together)
- Markers and crayons to draw the mural
- Hymnals or songbooks that contain the carol you will use to close
- Tape or CD system and recordings to play carols in #1
- Note cards and pencils for activity #6

OTHER PREPARATIONS

If you choose Option #6, clear a space so persons will not trip or fall over other furniture. Make this activity an "option" for those who for reason of age or health might find this activity too strenuous.

Leading the Session

GATHERING BY THE STAGE

1. If possible, play suggested carols for this week in the background before the session. Welcome adults as they enter.

2. Direct adults to the butcher paper or newsprint roll that will be used for the mural. Invite them to create a mural of scenes they associate with Advent and Christmas, both personal and biblical.

3. Display the completed mural. Allow persons to ask questions about and/or explain the scenes portrayed. Briefly discuss why Advent and Christmas might inspire or even require a variety of scenes to convey its meaning. Offer this or another prayer: *God of all creation, your coming among us does not always appear where we expect. Teach us to recognize your Advent no matter where we may be and to know in those places your grace and call. In the name of the Christ. Amen.*

EXPLORING THE STAGE'S DRAMA

4. Call attention to the four corners of the room where you have placed symbols of the scenes encountered in this week's readings. One corner at a time, invite adults to identify the scene represented, and how. Further identify the characters associated with that scene, and why.

   Option: Once all the corners and symbols have been identified and discussed, invite adults to decide silently which of those scenes they would most like to have been a part of and then physically go to that corner. Have each "corner" group discuss what led them to their choice. Share those ideas in summary with the larger group. If any corner went unchosen, discuss reasons why.

FINDING OURSELVES ONSTAGE

5. Move to the corner of the room where the "sitting room" has been set up. If that is not practical given the room and/or group size, bring the sitting room symbol(s) into the midst of the large group. Call on one or more of the participants to read Luke 1:24-25, 39-45, 56-57. Discuss Mary's and Elizabeth's patient waiting summarized there. Turn the conversation to the idea of the "sitting room" reviewed in that day's reading. Form small groups and discuss where and how persons find quiet places and times to wait and prepare for Advent's coming.

6. Move to the corner of the room of the inn or bring its

symbol(s) into the group area. Read Luke 2:7b. Ask adults to find partners and discuss what it feels like to be left out or told there is no room for them. Encourage adults to speak from personal experience, if they are comfortable doing so.

Option: Follow the discussion time with a game of musical chairs. Tell persons who are eliminated they must keep quiet until the game is over. Afterward, discuss what that game conveyed about the experience of exclusion.

Read the quote in the inn's reading from the Christmas sermon of Martin Luther. Ask persons whether they agree or disagree with Luther's assessment of how people today would have received Jesus back then, and why. Have adults silently and individually consider ways in which "Christ in your neighbor" can be made part of this Advent's preparations. Encourage persons to write down on a note card one action they will take because of this commitment during Advent.

7. Move to the corner representing the stable, or bring its symbol(s) into the group. Call attention to the mural created at the beginning of the session. Did any of the scenes involve animals? How? Identify any Advent or Christmas traditions in your church that involve animals, and for what purpose. Read the final three paragraphs in the stable reading. Ask the group to consider ways in which we keep such meanings alive in Advent and beyond.

8. Move to the corner representing the throne room, or bring its symbol(s) into the group. Read aloud Matthew 2:1-4, 7-8, 16a to the group. Invite adults to comment on what fears Herod brings to the scene, and how such fears continue to be played out in our lifetime. Ask the group to identify how your church addresses fears encountered in persons and in your community. Ask in closing: How do Advent and Christmas address the fears we have and the fears in our world, so that fear does not have the last word?

Wrap-Up

9. Elicit responses to what participants gained from this session and to questions raised by it.

10. Close by singing (or reading) "O Come, O Come, Emmanuel," or another of the carols suggested for this week.

11. Remind participants to read the next week's texts and readings and to listen to or use the carols as they are able.

Week Three: Gathering the Choruses

Session Preparation

PREPARE THE ROOM

This session calls for no special room preparation. If you choose, you may want to display some symbols of the four choruses, or even paper cutouts of the characters. Consider asking several members of the group to help you out with making these. If you go to the trouble of making them, incorporate them into one or more of the activities (such as, cluster the sheets created by the partners around each symbol or cutout).

MATERIALS NEEDED

- Hymnals or songbooks with the carol you will use for the closing

- Tape or CD system and recordings to play carols in #1 and #11

- Lined paper and pencils for activity #4

- Newsprint or markerboard and markers

If you choose the optional activity in #8, check with gift stores for small packets of frankincense and myrrh, as well as with Christian book or supply stores.

OTHER PREPARATIONS

If you light the frankincense and/or myrrh in optional activity in #8, you will need matches or lighter and some type of fireproof plate or holder on which to burn. Also, for safety, have an extinguisher or water available.

Leading the Session

GATHERING BY THE STAGE

1. Welcome adults as they enter. Play suggested carols from this week's readings in the background during the gathering time.

2. Ask adults, In this past week what have you heard of Advent/Christmas: where, from whom, and what was the "message"? Have adults call out responses, and record them on newsprint or markerboard. Use the resulting list to underscore the many voices or "choruses" (in the words of this week's readings) abroad in this season and the need for careful listening to discern their message to us. Affirm that this session will help us discern the message of the choruses of angels and shepherds, magi and innocents.

3. Offer this or another opening prayer: *God of grace and mystery, open us to hear anew your word of this season that speaks through the voices of others. In listening, may we truly hear; and in hearing, may we truly follow. In the name of the Christ who comes. Amen.*

EXPLORING THE STAGE'S DRAMA

4. Have adults choose partners. Give four sheets of paper to each set of partners. Draw a line down the center of each sheet vertically. Partners record on half the sheet what they believe is the key message for Advent brought by one of the choruses from this week's readings (angels, shepherds, magi, innocents)—one sheet for each chorus. In the other column they are to write one question that this chorus raises for them.

5. Post completed sheets around the room or on tables, and group the sheets according to the choruses represented. Have adults browse through all sheets to see what meanings and questions others found.

FINDING OURSELVES ONSTAGE

6. Read Luke 2:9-14. Ask adults whether angels make this story more or less accessible or believable to them, and why. Review the comments and questions on the partners' "angel" sheets, inviting adults to offer their insights into questions raised.

Option: Discuss as a group other places where angels appear in scripture, and the role angels seem to have in the mind of popular culture today. Compare and contrast the two.

Lead the discussion as to how those ideas about angels help or hinder receiving (and living) the message of peace and God's favor announced by the angels at Bethlehem.

7. Review and comment on the partners' sheets on the shepherds. Turn to the reading's emphasis on shepherds as outcasts. Ask adults to reflect on how the inclusion of outsiders remains part of our Advent preparations and Christmas observances, or seek suggestions for how individuals and the church might be more intentionally inclusive.

8. Read Matthew 2:1-12. Ask the group to identify how many of our popularly held ideas about the magi are actually part of the text. Review the partners' sheets on the magi in light of Matthew's text and the book's reading. Invite adults to imagine themselves as Joseph or Mary, asking them to respond to the gifts Joseph and Mary receive, especially one (myrrh) that is so closely associated with death.

Option: Pass around samples of frankincense and myrrh. Light one or more of the pieces of incense and allow each of the participants to smell the aroma. Relate the history of aroma as part of worship and its continued use in some branches of the Orthodox church today. You might also note that modern researchers now identify the sense of smell with some of our strongest memories. Ask group members to identify personal experiences where worship involved senses other than sight and hearing. Where and how does taste, touch, and/or smell enrich our experience in worship?

9. Read Matthew 2:12-18. Invite adults to stand for the following continuum exercise. Instruct adults who believe this story of the Innocents should be read every Christmas season to stand at one end of the room. Instruct those who

believe it should never be read during the Christmas season to stand at the opposite end of the room. Persons who believe something in between about the frequency of this story's use at Christmas, may position themselves accordingly. After persons have found their places, ask them why they stand where they do. Review the Innocents' sheets, both their meanings and questions, especially in light of the reading's idea of Herod's child victims dying in Jesus' place.

Option: Ask the group to identify the innocents at risk in this season: at risk from those whose seeking of power comes at any cost, at risk from sheer neglect, at risk from threats not easily identified. Ask the group to discuss ways in which individuals and/or the church can intervene on their behalf, to select one or two of those options, and to make them part of this Advent's preparations.

Wrap-Up

10. Invite adults' comments on the session about what they found helpful, what questions they still have, and what they gained from this time of learning and sharing. Incorporate their ideas in the next, and last, session.

11. Close by listening to or singing "Coventry Carol" or one of the other carols suggested from this week's readings. Offer a prayer of commissioning.

12. Remind adults to do the readings for the final chapter and next week's closing session.

Week Four: Casting the Central Characters

Session Preparation

PREPARE THE ROOM

Place one or more crèche sets in the worship area of your room or in some other visible location. In place of or in addition to the crèche set(s), bring in a manger used by your church for pageants or Christmas scenes.

MATERIALS NEEDED

- Newsprint sheets, markers
- Hymnals or songbooks with the carol you will use to close the session
- Audiocassette tape or CD system and recordings to play carols in #1
- Posterboard, magazines, scissors, and glue sticks

OTHER PREPARATIONS

If the optional "thank-you note" activity in #5 is used, provide thank-you notes (preferably with an Advent or Christmas motif) and pencils or pens.

Leading the Session

GATHERING BY THE STAGE

1. Welcome adults as they enter. Play suggested carols from this week's readings.

2. Instruct adults to create a group Advent collage, using both pictures and words or phrases from magazines. (For a large group, fasten together four pieces of posterboard, so all may work together.) Have them leave a large section in the center of the collage blank for the time being.

   When the collage is completed, talk about the words and pictures included. Ask what meanings or messages they convey for this season.

3. Use this or another prayer to open the session: *The waiting*

is nearly over, O God. Advent will soon be Christmas—but it is not yet so. Help us to see the characters take their places for the final scene and to understand the final preparations we can make by their example. We pray in the name of the Christ whose birth draws near and whose coming we await. Amen.

EXPLORING THE STAGE'S DRAMA

4. Form four small groups. Assign one of the characters from this week's readings to each group. Have each group discuss what its character brings to the Christmas stage and drama. Ask the groups to decide on one or more pictures and words or phrases to include in the collage as a summary of this discussion.

5. Have each group report to the others on its discussion and ideas with members adding pictures to the center of the collage as the report takes place.

   Option: Pass out thank-you notes and pens or pencils. Invite participants to write a thank-you note to one of these characters for a gift brought to this season, a gift of special importance to his or her faith and observance of this season.

FINDING OURSELVES ONSTAGE

6. Select three persons to read Luke 1:26-38 in parts: Mary, the angel, and a narrator. Invite others to imagine themselves in Mary's place. Afterward ask adults to discuss what struck them most about the role and especially the actions of Mary in this text: questioning, trusting, accepting. Identify ways in which Mary's responses continue to be part of our Advent preparations and expectations.

   Option: Those persons who wrote thank-you notes to Mary may read them aloud now.

7. Read to the group the opening two paragraphs from Day 3 on Joseph. Invite responses to the notion of dreams and dreamers in general and in regard to Joseph the betrothed

of Mary. Ask adults to identify the risks taken by Joseph in Matthew 1:18-25 and to consider how his risks parallel those faced by adults today.

Option: Those persons who wrote thank-you notes to Joseph may read them aloud now.

8. Look at the collage created earlier. Ask group members to identify where in those words and pictures they find "fulfillments" portrayed, talking about days in which persons connect Jesus' birth with the fulfilling of old and the making of new promises. Gather and seat the adults around the crèche set and/or manger. Ask them to think of the promise of fulfillment brought in the life of any new child and then of the gift brought by the manger child. Have them quietly reflect on the fulfillment brought in the manger while "What Child Is This" plays in the background.

Option: Those persons who wrote thank-you notes to the baby Jesus may read them aloud now.

9. Have one or more adults read Isaiah 42:14-16 and John 1:1-5, 14 aloud to the group. Invite adults to offer their understandings as to how these texts relate to the God who comes and speaks in Jesus' birth.

Option: Those persons who wrote thank-you notes to the God may read them aloud now.

Wrap-Up

10. Gather the adults once more around the crèche set(s) and/or manger, with those who are able standing. Invite persons to offer words about how these sessions have helped or shaped their experience of Advent and their preparations for Christmas. Thank the participants for the time they have shared by being part of this group.

11. Close by singing "Joy to the World."

Appendix Three

IDEAS FOR FAMILY AND CONGREGATIONAL OBSERVANCES

A dvent can provide families and congregations with special ways to mark the passage of time from Advent's preparations into Christmas's fulfillment. So how might this book serve as a resource for incorporating its ideas into such observances? The following thoughts and suggestions are organized according to the weeks of Advent. By no means feel, as families or a church, that all ideas must be employed for any to be used. Do what seems best to you in allowing this book to impact your observance of Advent most fruitfully. Pick and choose. Set the stage.

If it is possible in your congregation, coordinate some of the carols suggested for each week's readings with the carols to be sung during worship services that week. At home use whatever music playback systems you have to play some (or all) of the carols suggested. You may have some of these recordings in your personal collections of Christmas music. Others might be available through collections at local libraries. Others can be monitored on, if not downloaded from, the Internet (please respect all copyright laws when doing so). If you have children, finding Christmas carols on the Internet might help them realize that the computer's use can extend beyond fun, games, and homework.

Week One: Erecting the Backdrops

- List everything you plan to do this season that qualifies as preparation for Advent. Discuss ways in which responsibilities can be divided, so that all family members share the load. You might also consider matching every "busy" preparation with a spiritual preparation, such as reading from this book or setting aside a regular time for prayer.

- Ask your children what peace means to them and how they see Jesus' birth related to peace among persons as well as with God. Talk about ways your family can make peace more a part of this Advent.

AT CHURCH

- Consider commissioning a group to create four banners for your sanctuary during Advent, each based upon one of the prophets' words in this chapter. Or commission a single banner that will weave together symbols of all four of their messages. This same group (or others) might make one banner for each of the other chapters in the book. During the worship service in which each banner is first displayed, the children's time or the segment devoted to lighting the Advent candle can be used to interpret the banner's text and message.

- Encourage members of each church committee to spend as much time preparing themselves spiritually for this Advent as they do in carrying out the "business/busy-ness" of the season.

- Consider using a dramatic portrayal of one of the "messengers" of God, such as John the Baptizer, during one of the Advent worship services. The actor could simply read that day's scripture, present part or all of the sermon, or in some other way engage the congregation in an experience that tests abilities to listen to those God sends and to understand why their words sometimes go unheeded.

Week Two: Constructing the Scenery

- Designate one room, or some space in a room, as a quiet place for family members' use this Advent. As much as possible, free it from distractions. Leave in the room this book, a Bible, and perhaps other items or symbols of Advent that would help make it conducive to reflection and personal devotion. If you have children, explain what you are doing, and allow them to help you create that space. Encourage them both by your words and example to use it.

- If you have children, play a game of musical chairs. Talk with your children about their feelings when they get left out of the game because they don't have a chair. Use that experience to talk about what what Mary and Joseph might have felt when they found there was no room for them in Bethlehem.

- If you have small children, read one of the stories of the legends of the animals' speaking at midnight. Or take your children to a petting zoo (if one is open at this time of year) or a farm and remind them of Jesus' birth among the animals on Christmas.

At Church

- Set aside a room at church that will be available throughout Advent for personal meditation and devotion. A small worship center might include a table containing a candle or candles, one or more copies of this book, and a Bible. Next to the table, consider placing the manger your church may have in a closet or attic for pageants present or past. Encourage church members and friends to drop in during the week and to use this room throughout the season.

- If your church developed a single banner for the previous chapter, have another one made for this chapter, incorporating images of the places and scenes from these readings.

- Seek ways in which the sanctuary can be decorated gradually from one Sunday to the next through Advent, thus providing different scenes for the congregation's experience of Advent this year.

Week Three: Gathering the Choruses

At Home

- Display any crèche sets you may have. Depending on the fragility of your crèche sets, let your children touch them and even play with them (making sounds of the animals can be a fun activity for younger children). Talk with your children about the characters included in your crèche sets and why they are there. Encourage your children to ask one another who their favorite characters in the crèche are and why. If you do not have a crèche set, consider making a simple one out of paper or modeling clay.

- Encourage family discussion about how we learn of Advent and Christmas from various choruses today. For example, ask family members what they experience of this season from commercials on television, from carolers on the street, from bell ringers collecting for charities, or from your family's plans for this season. Ask how these choruses compare with those in the book.

At Church

- If possible, display your church's crèche set (if the church has one and if it fits) on the altar or Communion table. Use it with a children's sermon or candlelighting ceremony to draw attention to symbolism in the church. Consider gradually adding characters to the crèche over the four Sundays in Advent, adding the Christ Child at the Christmas Eve or Christmas Day service.

- Create a banner that will symbolize this week's choruses for use in worship.

- Write and use a choral reading on one of the Sundays in Advent, or even at your church's Christmas program, that incorporates the voices of the four choruses of this week's reading. One or more individuals could read each of the parts. The readers also could be costumed and/or staged in different areas of the chancel and sanctuary. To play the Innocents select children who would not be upset by the story they would be telling.

Week Four: Casting the Central Characters

At Home

- Write a letter of thanks to Joseph and Mary. If you have children, encourage them especially to explain why such thanks are in order. Also include in the letter questions you and your children would like to ask about the trip to Bethlehem, about the inn and the manger, or about the visits from angels each received.

- Paint or draw a picture of Jesus. Include around the picture symbols of the fulfillment Jesus brings. Help younger children understand that Jesus was born just as they were. You might want to get out baby pictures of them (or you!) to emphasize how Jesus came to life in the same way each one of us did.

- Talk about God's love that has come to us in Jesus' birth. Think of a gift of love your family can give to someone else as an expression of God's love.

At Church

- As part of a special Christmas program or the church coffee hour on the last Sunday before Christmas, plan a "visit" by Mary and Joseph during which persons may ask them questions. The two persons accepting such a role will need time to prepare for their appearance. Use costumes not of the biblical era but of two such persons in our own time. Make sure the "visit" ends with an opportunity for persons to express gratitude for the couple's trust and actions.

- Create and display a banner that includes the four central characters encountered in this chapter.

- In your church's main observance of Christmas (children's program, choral presentation, candlelight service, and/or Communion service), consider focusing the service's theme on the meaning of Christmas to God, using the chapter's reflections to spur the thoughts of those designing the service.

About the Author

John Indermark has lived in Naselle, Washington,
since 1984. John pastors a Methodist-Presbyterian
congregation in Raymond, along with writing
Christian education curriculum. This book is
his third, the previous two being *Genesis of Grace: A
Lenten Book of Days* and *Neglected Voices: Biblical
Spirituality in the Margins*. In their spare time, John and
his wife, Judy, enjoy traveling, beachcombing, flyfishing,
and working on their circa 1920s home. For the last
twelve years, John has been working on his version
of the Great American Novel.